The
Plant Community

Herbert C. Hanson

Research Professor of Ecology
Catholic University of America
Washington, D.C.

Ethan D. Churchill

Cornell Aeronautical Laboratory, Inc.
Combat Surveillance Project
Arlington, Virginia

Copyright © 1961 by
REINHOLD PUBLISHING CORPORATION
All rights reserved
Library of Congress Catalog Card Number: 61-10681
Printed in the United States of America

THIRD PRINTING, 1964

Printed in the United States of America
THE GUINN CO., INC.
New York 14, N. Y.

REINHOLD BOOKS IN
THE BIOLOGICAL SCIENCES

Consulting Editor:
PROFESSOR PETER GRAY

Department of Biological Sciences
University of Pittsburgh
Pittsburgh, Pennsylvania

The plant community is the heart and soul of any ecological system. Yet, surprisingly enough, it is often neglected in ecological texts since the animal community is so much more spectacular. I therefore welcome Dr. Hanson's and Dr. Churchill's book to the *Reinhold Books in the Biological Sciences* as a book which will make plant ecology exciting to any reader. Though the book is intended as a text for a short course, it cannot fail to interest anyone concerned with the maintenance and development of life on this planet.

Unlike many contemporary ecological texts, this work does not neglect taxonomy in theory or practice, so that the reader starts with a clear realization of the role of a species in helping to build a community, and goes from there to an understanding of the community as a functional entity.

The authors have drawn not only from their own wide experience of many natural environments but also from the whole field of ecological literature to build a book which offers a fresh, well-integrated approach to a subject which should be of universal interest.

February, 1961   PETER GRAY

To
EDITH and LOU

PREFACE

The study of vegetation requires the fullest possible knowledge of the basic units—the plant communities. In an effort to promote this knowledge and to advance the science of vegetation, the authors have adopted as the central theme of this book the formation and nature of the plant community. The development of the theme begins with a discussion of the properties of species and populations, i.e., of the relations of plants and animals to their physical environment and to one another. It is then demonstrated how these properties lead to the formation of various kinds of groupings and communities. This discussion is followed by an analysis of community characteristics and their use in description and classification, and of the changes, or dynamics, that occur in plant communities. Numerous illustrative examples are provided in order to clarify concepts and to assist in the solution of specific problems, particularly as they are encountered in the field.

This book is intended as a text for semester or quarter courses in plant ecology; as a supplement to textbooks in general ecology which usually do not deal adequately with the formation and nature of the plant community; or as an adjunctive text for courses in animal ecology, forestry, range management, wildlife management, conservation, and agriculture. It is also intended to serve the general reader who desires to be better informed about the nature of vegetation and its potentialities.

The background for the ideas expressed in the following pages is a mosaic of varied kinds of experience. Contributions to this mosaic have been drawn from the fertile field of ecological literature; from field work on vegetation in desert scrub, grasslands, forests, and tundra; from publications of the authors; and from many years devoted to teaching courses in plant and general ecology. The authors were inspired by men who have contributed much to the development of ecology, including F. E. Clements, J. E. Weaver, G. E. Nichols, V. E. Shelford, and C. C. Adams.

The authors are also greatly indebted to Jack Major, Warren C. Whitman, R. H. Whittaker, Peter Gray, James B. Ross, and Dorothy Donath for reading the manuscript and offering many helpful suggestions, criticisms, and comments.

HERBERT C. HANSON
ETHAN D. CHURCHILL

Washington, D.C.
Arlington, Virginia
February, 1961

CONTENTS

PART THREE
Dynamics of Communities

PART FOUR
Classification of Communities

INTRODUCTION

The study of vegetation or of plant communities is concerned with the ecology or interrelationships of plants and animals to one another and to the environment; and also with their composition and structure, genesis, chorology, history, dynamics and classification. In this viewpoint the community is the focus and ecology is one kind of approach.

The individual plant requires not only light to provide energy for photosynthesis, but a suitable temperature, carbon dioxide, water, certain minerals, and chlorophyll. Photosynthesis, as is true also of all other functions of the plant, is dependent upon a number of external and internal conditions. Neighboring plants may reduce the light intensity so much that a seedling pine may not be able to grow, or fundamental damage may be caused by leaf-destroying insects. The individual plant in order to live must establish successful relations with its physical environment as well as with other plants and animals.

In nature plants usually grow in groups, not as isolated individuals. These groups may consist of plants of a single species, constituting a population, but more often the groups comprise individuals of several species, constituting a community. A great deal is known about the ecology of individual organisms, the ecological relationships of populations are now being intensively studied, and much work has been done on communities as well. It has been suggested that communities of interacting populations may also behave as units in natural selection.[45] These three levels of ecological integration, the individual, the population, and the community, are considered in the study of ecology.

Seeds of many kinds of plants are carried into bare areas, where many of the seeds germinate; but only those that are suited to the prevailing conditions will grow and produce offspring. The kinds of plants that can grow in a particular habitat must have the ability to grow not only under the prevailing physical environmental conditions, but also in association and competition with neighboring plants. Some species are more successful than others, as shown by the number, size, or behavior of the individuals. Hence the potentialities of species, differing according to their genetic constitutions, determine not only the types of habitats that each can occupy, but also the nature of the interrelationships that develop with other species. These potentialities furnish the key to understanding how groupings are formed, the nature of the groupings or communities, the processes occurring within them, and how one kind of community can replace another. The complexity of the community and the intricate relationships of organisms to one another and to the environment, therefore, depend upon the habits and qualities of individual species; hence knowledge of the latter will aid us in understanding the community as a whole. When interrelations of the individual species are emphasized, the study is often called **autecology,** in contrast to **synecology,** the study of the community ecology. The former is obviously incomplete because different kinds of plants live together.

In this book the nature of the species in relation to the physical environment and in relation to other organisms will be treated first because knowledge of the organism is essential to understanding the formation and maintenance of communities. This will be followed by a discussion of the ecological success of a species. The formation of groups or communities and their characteristics and dynamics will then be treated, and the nature of the climax community considered. The final portion of the book will deal with the classification of communities.

PART ONE

Species and Populations

1

ECOLOGICAL CHARACTERISTICS OF SPECIES AND POPULATIONS

The ways in which plants carry on their life processes, developed and genetically fixed during the course of evolution of each kind, differ from species to species. The genetic constitution of each species does permit a certain range of expression or functioning according to the species and the impinging environmental conditions. Some plants, for example, can bloom and produce seed in the shade, others require full sunlight. Some can carry on photosynthesis and grow under a wide range of soil moisture conditions, others require a continuously saturated soil. Legumes can utilize the nitrogen fixed by bacteria in their root nodules, while most species must secure their nitrogen from the soil.

These ways of carrying on life processes are a fundamental part of the characteristics of the species and determine in large measure the formation of groups of organisms or communities. The physical and the biotic influences interact upon one another, so it is often difficult to determine the most important relationships that influence success. Furthermore, species differ genetically in plasticity; some kinds are readily modified in regard to characters such as size, number, and structure of leaves, or number of seeds; other kinds are much more rigidly fixed. The principles may be outlined as follows:

(1) Relations of species to the physical environment:
  (a) Every species has certain essential requirements,
  (b) Every species possesses ecological amplitude, i.e., a characteristic potentiality for growth within a limited range of environmental conditions,
  (c) Every species has a characteristic capacity for utilizing the available resources of the environment in which it occurs.
(2) Relations among individuals of the same or of different species. Species differ in the following ways:
  (a) In competitive capacity,
  (b) In capacity of association,
  (c) In reproductive processes,
  (d) In resistance to grazing, mowing, or other treatment,
  (e) In susceptibility to parasites,
  (f) In mutualistic and commensal relationships.

The ecological success of a species depends upon its capacity to cope with the physical environment and with associated species in the relationships stated in the above principles.

RELATIONS OF SPECIES TO THE PHYSICAL ENVIRONMENT

The physical environment is a complex of factors which may be classified into three rather arbitrary groups: (1) **climatic factors,** which include light, heat or cold, precipitation, humidity, wind, gases, and evaporating power of the air; (2) **soil factors,** which include texture, structure, depth, and ingredients such as water, gases, mineral constituents, acidity, alkalinity, and salinity; (3) **topographic factors,** which include the degree, extent, and direction of slope, relief, and altitude, ground water, and snow accumulation or removal (Figure 1-1). Fire, although often caused by man, may also be included under climatic factors, but

Figure 1-1. Climatic, topographic, and biotic factors all play a part in determining the various kinds of subalpine and alpine vegetation. Several sharp community boundaries are evident here. Sheep are searching for the more tender parts of plants in the high Sawtooth Valley in Idaho. September, 1958. (U.S.D.A. Soil Conservation Service.)

because of its importance it may well be classified separately.

Some of these factors, particularly water, light, humidity, heat and cold, mineral nutrients, and gases, affect plants directly. Wind, soil texture and structure, and precipitation usually influence plants indirectly through the direct factors. Physiographic factors are more remote, for they affect the indirect factors which in turn influence the direct factors; for example, an increase in elevation may cause greater precipitation which in turn increases the soil moisture. The response of plants is often related to periodicity, such as summer and winter periods of precipitation, and to the ranges and fluctuations in various phases, rather than to average values.

Each environmental factor has two or sometimes three phases: intensity, duration, and quality. High intensity of heat accompanied by low humidity causes more damage if the duration covers several days rather than a few hours. Light possesses three phases. The intensity of light varies from 8000 to 10,000 foot candles at noon on a clear day in the open to as low as 100 foot candles in a dense forest. The duration of light influences the blooming of some kinds of plants; thus some bloom when the days are short, others when the days are long. The quality of light affects photosynthesis, the red rays being most effective in this process.

Plants respond to a complex of environmental factors impinging upon them simultaneously, and it is often difficult to segregate one particular factor as causing a certain response. Transpiration, for example, is influenced by heat, humidity, soil moisture, light, wind, and other factors all operating at the same time. On a south-facing slope the rate of transpiration is usually greater than on a north-facing one because of the greater intensity of several of these factors. At the same time that the rate of transpiration is increasing as the heat and wind become more intense, other processes such as photosynthesis, absorption, translocation, assimilation, and growth are also being affected. Every habitat has a different combination of environmental factors—the complex in a forest, for example, differing considerably from that in a grassland. While both the environment and the community are complex, it needs to be emphasized that the community represents an especially high degree of complexity because it is made up of individual organisms, each functioning in its own particular way in relation to an environment in which one factor may be critical at one time, and another at some other time. Thus in a certain spot one plant with a shallow root system may be wilting while a deep-rooted plant in the same spot is flourishing, but in early spring, when the surface soil is moist, the former may be growing rapidly, the latter slowly.

Essential Requirements for Every Species

The basic needs for survival, such as water, mineral nutrients, light, and heat must be available, or the plant cannot live and grow. For example, the U-3 strain of Bermudagrass (*Cynodon dactylon*) requires more than 1232 degree-hours (summation of degrees above 0°F per hour per day) and day temperatures above 50°F to show measurable growth. If the night temperature falls below 50°, the day temperature must be correspondingly higher to raise the number of degree-hours to the essential minimum.[213]

Aquatic plants (**hydrophytes**) such as the water-lily (*Nymphaea*) and the submerged eel-grass (*Zostera*) require a continuous supply of water; in contrast are numerous desert plants such as the creosote bush (*Larrea divaricata*), prickly pear (*Opuntia*), and others (**xerophytes**) which are able to endure long periods without rain. Many annuals in the Arizona desert flourish during the cool weeks of late winter and early spring when the rainfall has been adequate. In the Great Plains, western wheatgrass (*Agropyron smithii*) requires more moisture and less heat for good growth than buffalograss (*Buchloe dactyloides*), and by the same token, for the germination of seeds and later growth of many species the soil moisture must be adequate at the periods of the year when the temperatures are suitable. Some grasses, notably the sixweeks grasses (*Sporobolus microspermus, Festuca octoflora, Bouteloua barbata, B. parryi, Aristida adscensionis*), can grow and mature during the summer in southern Arizona when soil moisture is available for only a short time. Many kinds of weeds grow in size in almost direct relation to the supply of available soil moisture, Russian thistle (*Salsola kali*), for example, growing from only an inch or two to as much as two feet with a spread of as many feet or more, in response to different amounts of soil moisture. In addition, an insufficient depth of soil may prevent development of the root system of some deep-rooted grasses such as orchardgrass (*Dactylis glomerata*), leaving the area open to invasion by shallow-rooted grasses or weedy plants.

An adequate supply of mineral nutrients in the soil, including the trace elements, is most important for the growth of plants. This phase of physiology is very inadequately understood for wild plants, but the decline in vigor of some species that apparently have high nutritional requirements, especially in grasslands suffering from heavy grazing or erosion, permitting the invasion of

Figure 1-2. A plant with wide ecological amplitude, side-oats gramagrass (*Bouteloua curtipendula*), is a leafy, perennial bunchgrass widely distributed from California to Montana, Maine, and South Carolina, being most abundant in the Great Plains. August, Texas. (U.S.-D.A. Soil Conservation Service.)

species with lower requirements, points to mineral deficiency as a cause. Areas in the vicinity of bird roosts and animal dens or burrows may favor the persistence or the invasion of species with high nitrogen requirements—for optimum growth many grasses need more nitrate and phosphate than is naturally present in some soils. Sufficient potash in relation to nitrogen has been found to reduce the winterkilling of some grasses, while lime is often needed in some soils to counteract acidity. The trace elements, boron, copper, manganese, or zinc, may be required to remedy soil deficiencies in some regions.

Big sagebrush (*Artemisia tridentata*) and its common associates are practically never found in soils developed from altered volcanic rocks in the western part of the Great Basin in the United States. Apparently these plants are unable to secure some essen-

Figure 1-3. Essential requirements are not adequate for corn on this hill; grassland would not only make better use of the resources but also improve them. Michigan. (U.S.D.A. Soil Conservation Service.)

tial requirements, for the soils there are quite acid and very deficient in phosphorus, nitrogen, and exchangeable bases compared to soils from unaltered rocks where *Artemisia tridentata* and its associates grow. The pines, *Pinus ponderosa* and *P. jeffreyi,* and some herbaceous montane plants are able to grow in mineral-deficient soils, however, even though the precipitation is considerably less than in the pine forests of the Sierra Nevada Mountains to the west.[13]

Many grasses possess definite length-of-day requirements. A strain of side-oats gramagrass (*Bouteloua curtipendula*) (Figure 1-2) from southern Texas requires intermediate or short days, with an upper critical photoperiod of 13 to 14 hr, for vigorous growth. A strain of this same grass from North Dakota requires long days, flowering vigorously in day lengths of more than 14 hr—even vegetative growth of this strain being severely limited when the photoperiod is below 13.5 hr. Plants from central Oklahoma have either intermediate or long-day requirements, with a lower critical photoperiod of less than 13 hr, vegetative growth of this strain being vigorous in periods of 13 hr or more.[156] By means of this ecotypic differentiation in essential requirements, side-oats grama is adapted to a wide latitudinal range. Little bluestem (*Andropogon scoparius*) shows an even wider adaptation of requirements to latitudinal and other environmental conditions. Thus in the reseeding of depleted lands it is important to consider the requirements of the strains or species that are used. The seed should come from areas as similar as possible, especially in latitude, temperature, precipitation, and evaporating power of the air. Such similar areas are known as **homoclimes** or **agroclimatic analogs.**[152]

Knowledge of the requirements of cultivated plants is far advanced in contrast to that for wild plants (Figure 1-3). The former are usually grown in single cultures under definite spacing so that competition between plants for essential requirements is reduced sufficiently to permit maximum yields per acre. Wild plants, however, grow in mixtures of many species in which it is difficult to determine the requirements of individual ones. Data obtained by growing wild plants in pure cultures are only partially applicable to natural mixtures because of great differences in requirements, as indicated by differences in growth rate and form, when they are grown in association. Techniques for determining the requirements of species in natural stands need to be designed, so the effects of competition and other interactions may be better understood.

Ecological Amplitude

The characteristic potentiality for growth of a species within a limited range of environmental conditions is known as the **ecological amplitude** or **tolerance range** of the species. Ecological amplitude seems preferable because it presents more clearly the idea of the range of conditions in which an organism can live and thrive, while tolerance refers more to the extremes within which an organism can survive. The former is affirmative and definite, the latter is negative. In his "Theory of Tolerance and Principle of Limiting Factors," Good emphasizes that plant distribution is controlled primarily by climatic factors, secondarily by edaphic factors; that plant processes are limited by definite ranges of intensity of climatic and edaphic factors; and that the range of amplitude for a particular factor often differs for various stages of the life cycle.[92]

The ecological amplitude of a species depends upon the genetic variability, or the array of biotypes and ecotypes that it possesses, as well as upon the range of phenotypic expression of the biotypes and ecotypes. For example, *Stipa spartea* owes its range of ecological amplitude to broad phenotypic expression of one or a few kinds of genotypes, but *Andropogon scoparius* owes its wide range to many kinds of ecotypes, each one with its own individual range of phenotypic expression.[140] The ecological amplitude of many species is apparently not only wide enough for it to live in its usual habitat, but also to live if necessary in habitats that are less favorable. This reserve of amplitude is similar to Nicholson's idea of "hyperadaptation" produced by natural selection[150] and to McMillan's "fund of genetic insurance . . . which would enable survival of a population under changed habitat conditions." [140] The survival in a somewhat different environment from the original one may provide a base for further ecological adaptation. On the other hand, while the amplitude may be wide enough for survival in the physical conditions of the new habitat, competition with other organisms better adapted to this environment may prevent survival.

The ecological amplitude of a species is often decisive in determining whether or not it will be present in a certain habitat or community. It is also often decisive in determining the endurance of a species to fluctuations in the environment within a certain habitat. In the long course of evolution some species have become attuned to the amplitudes of cold regions, others to those of hot regions, saline deserts, or temperate forests. At least one, but usually more, environmental factors may be critical in limiting the ecological amplitude of a species so that it is restricted in its geographical distribution. Kentucky bluegrass (*Poa pratensis*), for example, is limited in its southward distribution, chiefly, it appears, by high summer temperatures and low, or excessive, soil moisture. Bermudagrass (*Cynodon dactylon*) is limited northward by low intensity or insufficient duration of adequate temperatures. The former has a wide range of amplitude at lower temperatures, the latter a wide range at higher temperatures. But Bermudagrass appears to have a wider range for soil moisture than Kentucky bluegrass.

TABLE 1-1. AMPLITUDES OF SPECIES TO APPROXIMATE CONCENTRATIONS OF MINERAL SALTS IN MARSH, TRANSITION BOG, AND SPHAGNUM BOG IN CENTRAL RUSSIA. (After N. J. Katz.[121])

Marsh, 6 to 10%	Transition Bog, 5 to 6%	Sphagnum Bog, 3.5 to 5%
	Pinus	*silvestris*
Betula	*alba*	*Scheuchzeria palustris*
Alnus glutinosa	*Carex lasiocarpa*	*Rhynchospora alba*
	Carex	*limnosa*
Carex	*rostrata*	*Eriophorum vaginatum*
Menyanthes trifoliata		*Ledum palustre*
Calla palustris		*Cassandra calyculata*
Carex vesicaria		
Carex diandra	*Molinia coerulea*	
Carex gracilis	*Calamagrostis lanceolata*	
Carex paradoxa		
Carex caespitosa		
Aulocomnium palustre		
Camptothecium nitens	*Sphagnum subbicolor*	*Sphagnum medium*
Acrocladium cuspidatum		*Sphagnum balticum*
Drepanocladus vernicosus	*Sphagnum*	*recurvum*

In rigorous environments the geographic distribution of species is probably indicative of tolerance limits. For example, in Spitzbergen, species such as *Luzula confusa, Oxyria digyna, Polygonum vivipara, Poa alpina vivipara, Salix polaris,* and *Saxifraga oppositifolia* which grow in a variety of habitats differing in altitude and substratum, probably have wide ecological amplitudes, while other species such as *Alopecurus alpinus, Calamagrostis neglecta, Carex mis-*

andra, Trisetum spicatum, Silene acaulis, Pedicularis hirsuta, and *Draba oblongata* which grow in one or a few kinds of habitats seem to have narrow ranges.[174] Competition may, however, play some role in the distribution of these species. In central Russia *Menyanthes tri-foliata* occurs as a dominant in a number of marsh and bog communities in part because of its wide range of ecological amplitude with respect to water, concentration of mineral salts, and light intensity, as shown in Table 1-1. *Pinus silvestris* can grow where the water-table is 15 to 20 cm below the soil surface, but it is not dominant unless the water-table is about twice that deep.[121]

Zonation of plants is often caused by differences in ecological amplitude of species. The causative factor may be the water content of the substratum, as on the borders of lakes; salt content of the soil, as in saline depressions; or length of the growing season, as on mountain peaks (Figure 1-4). The duration of snow cover in arctic and alpine regions affects the length of the growing season and the amount of soil moisture. For example, in the bottom of a small alpine valley in Rondane, Norway, where the snow melts late, the ground is covered with meadow-like vegetation, with *Deschampsia flexuosa* and *Carex bigelowii* as herbaceous domi-

Figure 1-4. Variation in environmental conditions, with increasing altitude and differences between species in requirements and ecological amplitude, are causes of zonation. The zones shown here are (1) foreground, 8000 to about 9000 ft: low shrubs (*Gutierrezia, Chrysothamnus*) and blue grama-grass (*Bouteloua gracilis*); (2) oak brush to about 9500 ft; (3) spruce-fir to about 11,500 ft, with much aspen in old burns; (4) alpine to about 12,500 ft. West-facing slopes of the Sangre de Cristo Range, Colorado.

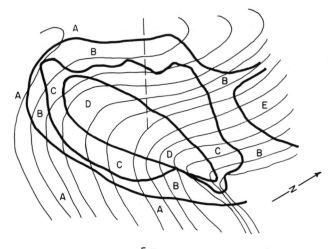

5 m

Chart 1. Chart of snow-bed vegetation at altitude of 1090 m in the Rondane Region, Norway, occurring as zones because of the response of species to depth and duration of snow cover. Community boundaries are shown in heavy lines, relief in light form-lines. (See Chart 2 for frequency distribution of species along transect shown in broken line.) (A) *Cetrarietum nivalis;* (B) *Cladonietum alpestris-Betuletosum;* (C) *Myrtilletum dicranetosum;* (D) *Deschampsieto-Dicranetum fuscae;* (E) *Phyllodoco-Juncetum trifidi.* (After Dahl, E. (62), "Rondane, Mountain Vegetation in South Norway and Its Relation to the Environment," Figure 9, Aschehoug & Co., Oslo, 1956.)

nants and the moss *Dicranum fuscescens* and the hepatic *Orthocaulis floerkei* making up most of the ground cover. A dark-colored, low shrub zone occupies the lower parts of the slopes, with *Vaccinium myrtillus* as the chief dominant and having the same ground cover as in the preceding area (see Charts 1 and 2). The next higher zone is light-colored, consisting mostly of the lichen *Cladonia alpestris.* On top of the ridge where the snow cover is lacking or thin and melts early, the lichens are chiefly *Cetraria nivalis* and *Alectoria ochroleuca.*[62] Some species grow where the snow lasts long and hence it appears that their amplitude range is narrow, while other species such as *Vaccinium myrtillus,* growing where the snow cover is medium in depth, have a fairly wide range. The lichen

Cetraria islandica has an extremely wide range. Competition is also involved in the zonation for certain species such as *Cladonia alpestris,* and other lichens do not grow well in close association with taller vascular plants.

Zonation along seacoasts is often caused by differential tolerance of species to salinity. Salt spray appears to be the chief factor in causing zonation on the Atlantic Coast of the southeastern United States. Adjacent to the bare beach is a zone of sea oats (*Uniola paniculata*) forming a foredune, followed inland by a zone

Chart 2. Frequency distribution of species along the transect shown in Chart 1. Communities are indicated by letters A, B, C, and D. (After Dahl, E. (62), "Rondane, Mountain Vegetation in South Norway and Its Relation to the Environment," Figure 10, Aschehoug & Co., Oslo, 1956.)

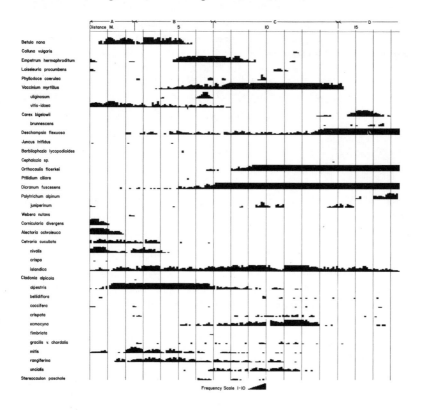

Figure 1-5. The ecological amplitude of cypress (*Taxodium distichum*) enables it to grow in shallow water. May, North Carolina. (U. S. Forest Service.)

of wax myrtle (*Myrica cerifera*) and yaupon (*Ilex vomitoria*), which is finally succeeded inland by a zone of maritime live oak (*Quercus virginiana*) on the stable dunes. All the zones are exposed to salt spray, the sea oats receiving the most.[21]

Phenological differences, such as the appearance of flowers in species at different seasons of the year, are usually caused by variations in ecological amplitude. Annual species in California deserts have definite and rather narrow limits of amplitude for the amount and duration of precipitation and for temperature conditions while the soil is wet, some species germinating and growing only in the summer, others only in the winter.[120]

Plants growing within the optimum range of ecological amplitude of the species (Figure 1-5) can be expected to be best in vigor and in greatest density, but even under such conditions competition may have detrimental effects. Usually a species possesses maximum competitive power in a habitat that is in the optimum range. However, as the limits of the amplitude range are approached, the plants become increasingly susceptible to loss of vigor and death, partly because of competition with other species.

Figure 1-6. Rapid growth, dense cover, and soil-binding roots with nitrogen-fixing bacteria, make kudzu (*Pueraria thunbergiana*) valuable in erosion control in the southeastern United States. October, Mississippi. (U.S.D.A. Soil Conservation Service.)

The influence, or reactions, of a species upon the habitat may produce optimum conditions for the same or for other species. Cattail (*Typha*), for example, when it first invades a lake improves the habitat for itself, but later, as the soil level is raised, the habitat becomes more suitable for invaders. Cycles of changes may occur (see Chapter 4) as in Great Britain with *Festuca ovina* as the key plant. It invades stony areas, improves the soil, and forms hummocks, which gradually increase in height causing the fescue to lose vigor. Lichens then invade and erosion follows, resulting in a stony surface again. The cycle includes a building phase and a degenerative phase, in which the reactions of the plants change the environmental conditions from poor to good and then to poor again for the respective species. These changes and the differences in ecological amplitude make the cycle possible.[197]

Some species have more pronounced reactions than others, and this may be of considerable importance in soil improvement (Figure 1-6). In Nebraska the cool-season grasses: *Agropyron desertorum, A. intermedium, A. smithii, A. cristatum, Bromus inermis,* and *Elymus junceus,* after seven years' growth, had a more favorable effect on the soil structure, permitting greater penetration of water, than the warm-season grasses: *Andropogon gerardi, Bouteloua curtipendula, B. gracilis,* and *Buchloe dactyloides.* An additional factor was involved in the low intake of water where *Buchloe* was growing, for the numerous fine roots entrapped air bubbles thus reducing the infiltration.[146]

Efficiency of Species in Utilizing the Available Resources of the Environment

This efficiency is attributable to the genetically induced effectiveness, under various environmental conditions, of physiological processes, which are summed or integrated in the principles concerning requirements and the ecological amplitude. Many annual species have greater capacity than perennials for growth on depleted sites in early stages of succession, apparently because of their wide ecological amplitude, great plasticity in size, and small requirements, but it appears that the plants in the early stages

Figure 1-7. Russian thistle (*Salsola kali*) is efficient in utilizing resources of various habitats from drought-stricken fields and grasslands to embryonic dune areas. Note dust storm in distance. March, near Fremont, Wyoming. (U.S.D.A. Soil Conservation Service.)

Figure 1-8. While soil requirements of grassland, chief species needle-and-thread (*Stipa comata*), must be secured in deep soil with relatively few rocks, those of mountain mahogany (*Cercocarpus montanus*) can be obtained in a very rocky substratum. August, Front Range, Colorado.

usually make less use of the environmental resources than those in the later stages (Figure 1-7).

Considerable variation exists between species in capacity to utilize resources of the habitat (Figure 1-8). For example, *Bromus inermis* and *Agropyron smithii* show greater response to nitrate fertilizer than *Bouteloua gracilis* under similar conditions, and in northern Colorado *Stipa viridula* and *Agropyron smithii* renew spring growth earlier than *Bouteloua gracilis, Buchloe dactyloides,* and *Aristida longiseta.* Vegetative growth of these species is usually completed by the latter part of June when the soil moisture has been exhausted, but *Buchloe* and *Bouteloua* are able to renew growth readily later in the summer if rains provide enough soil moisture; *Agropyron* and *Stipa,* however, cannot grow well at the higher temperatures. In western North Dakota the well-adapted species: *Agropyron smithii, Stipa comata, Bouteloua gracilis, Carex eleocharis,* and

Figure 1-9. Variations in size and shape of cones and in scale characters are found in natural stands of slash pine (*Pinus caribaea*), the state tree of Alabama. Florida. (U. S. Forest Service.)

C. pennsylvanica produce more than 60 per cent of their vegetative growth by the end of July. It is evident that during the evolution of grasslands in the Great Plains, natural selection has resulted in producing a high degree of adaptiveness to rigorous and variable environmental conditions.

Within a single stand, even a very homogeneous one, individuals of each species probably differ slightly in their minimum requirements of water and other substances and in their ranges of ecological amplitude. Moreover, variations in environmental conditions produce microhabitats in even the most uniform stands. The population of a species within a given microhabitat may belong to one genotype, constituting a **biotype,** while neighboring microhabitats contain other biotypes. In this way the various clusters of biotypes, within one species, occupying a particular kind of habitat, constitute an **ecotype.**[109] The number and kinds of biotypes vary according to kinds of species and habitats, so a remarkable genetic diversity exists in both natural and cultivated populations[68] (Figures 1-9 and 1-10). A number of transplant experiments have shown that the relationship of the ecotype to conditions of the original habitat is close, and so long as the conditions remain within a critical range, one kind of ecotype will prevail. But if the conditions change beyond this range, then it can be expected that a sorting of biotypes will lead to an increase in the better-adapted kinds and a decrease or disappearance of others, resulting in time in a new ecotype, and consequently in increased capacity to grow under changed conditions.

New biotypes apparently can readily form when plants are grown in a new habitat for a few generations. Strains of forage plants, for example, from a northern latitude, when grown for two or three generations in more southern latitudes, show increased susceptibility to frost and decreased production of green forage when grown again in the north.[188] Therefore, in hastening the production of seed of a new strain by growing it in a more favorable region, the length of time in this region should be limited to one or two generations at the most, so natural selection of new biotypes will not modify the characteristics of the strain.

Hybridization also produces new types that may be more efficient than the parents in utilizing the resources of the environment. Habitat preferences are inherited in substantially the same fashion as any other character, so many hybrids are unlikely to

Figure 1-10. Genetic diversity in height, leafiness, date of maturity, and seed production is shown in strains of Canada wildrye growing in an observational nursery, Pullman, Washington. (U.S.D.A. Soil Conservation Service.)

survive in nature because suitable habitats are usually not available, unless the natural vegetation has been disturbed.[3] Natural hybridization between species in the same genus, and even between species in different genera, is more common in the grass family than in most families of flowering plants, probably because grasses usually grow close together, are wind-pollinated, and many kinds are self-incompatible.[182] Parents differing considerably in requirements and amplitude are likely to produce hybrids which possess broad adaptation. In artificial breeding it is important that both parents have ranges of requirements and amplitude which approach the environmental conditions of the area where the hybrid is to be grown, for example, species adapted to the southwestern part of the Great Plains, where winters are cold and dry and the summers hot with frequent showers in late summer, are not suitable as parents of hybrids to be used in parts of California with cool, rainy winters and hot, dry summers.[40] It has been found, however, that the genetic systems of some wild species can be rearranged through interspecific crossings so that the modified amplitude of the offspring enables them to live in various habitats.[29]

RELATIONS AMONG INDIVIDUALS OF THE SAME OR DIFFERENT SPECIES

The complexity in the interrelations of plants is caused by the number, variety, and frequency of interactions between many individuals. The interactions change with the time of day and with the season; some are favorable for growth and reproduction, some are unfavorable, and some appear inconsequential. These interrelations have been grouped under various terms such as **symbiosis** in a broad sense,[139,70] **coaction,**[43] and types of reactions or **interactions.**[155] A useful classification of interrelations on the basis of contiguity is as follows:

(1) Interrelations of organisms that are not in actual contact or not in contact continuously; disjunctive.

(2) Interrelations of organisms that are in close bodily contact, where, if this contact is broken, one or the other organism suffers; conjunctive.

Some disjunctive interrelations are competition, association of species, pollination, dispersal of seeds and fruits, antibiosis, and grazing. Conjunctive interrelations include parasitism, mutualism, and commensalism.

The interrelations of species as they affect the grouping of organisms will be considered under six principles, four disjunctive and two conjunctive.

Differences of Species in Competitive Capacity

Competition is the state or relationship that exists between individuals of the same or different species when the resources of the ecosystem in which they are living are insufficient to supply the needs of all the plants in it. In a rigorous sense, "competition" is not the most precise term. In a soil where the water content is approaching the wilting percentage, the plants with deeper roots or superior water economy may continue to live until more water comes; the wilting and death of many plants are caused by insufficient soil moisture, not by any direct action of one plant upon another.[44] The term "competition," as usually used, refers to the greater growth in vigor of some individuals as compared to others when a certain requirement is in short supply for one or more individuals. The capacity to compete depends upon the requirements, ecological amplitude, and efficiency in resource use of the various biotypes in an area.

Many qualities, both genotypic and phenotypic, influence the competitive capacity of plants. Some of these are rate of growth, size, ability to produce tillers, tolerance of drought or shade, annual or perennial habit of growth, and the number of leaves and roots. The plants that are most efficient in utilizing resources in short supply have the best chance of survival, but even under severe competition some less efficient biotypes will survive because of their location in more favorable microhabitats. Adaptations such as a shallow root system and early spring growth that reduce competition with other deep-rooted, summer-growing species enable some species to survive.

Competition between individuals of closely similar competitive capacity, as within an ecotype population, is very intense in thick stands of seedlings of young plants (Figure 1-11). The struggle for

Figure 1-11. Competition is intense between individuals of one species, the red pine (*Pinus resinosa*), in this 25-year-old stand. Minnesota. (U. S. Forest Service.)

existence results in a pattern in which the spacing of the survivors is adapted in high measure to the resources of the environment, e.g., bunchgrasses which are more closely spaced in mesic than in xeric sites. When two species of the same genus, occurring in the same region, are very similar in growth-form and phenology, such as *Andropogon scoparius* and *A. virginicus* in the southeastern United States, they do not usually occur together in the same stand in similar spacing or abundance. One is usually numerous, the other sparse, indicating that there must be differences in requirements or ecological amplitude not evident in the gross life-form or phenology, which give one the advantage in competition over the other in certain habitats. These differences may explain in part why associated plants usually belong to different genera, for then they are more likely to be sufficiently dissimilar in requirements and amplitudes so they can associate without competing. One species may grow well in the shade of another because of differences in light requirements, another species may absorb water and nutrients at a different level or at a different

Figure 1-12. Competition may be severe between plants of different life-form, such as grasses and mesquite (*Prosopis*). When the latter is killed the grasses increase in vigor. In this late-summer aspect, grasses are dominant in the foreground, mesquite in the background. September, Santa Rita Experimental Range, southern Arizona. (U. S. Forest Service.)

time. The requirements of species in various genera usually differ more in time and space than species in the same genus, but this is not invariably true (Figure 1-12); differences in either case may be so great that they cannot grow in the same habitat. On the other hand, species in different genera such as *Bouteloua gracilis* and *Buchloe dactyloides* in parts of the central Great Plains, undergo competition similar to that between individuals of the same species; and in some habitats species in the same genus, such as *Bouteloua gracilis* and *B. curtipendula,* are associated apparently because the resources of the environment are adequate to supply the somewhat different needs of each and because the genetic individuality of each is not lost in hybridization. Much more field and experimental research is needed for understanding the association or lack of it between similar and dissimilar species.

A species can be expected to have greatest competitive capacity when it is growing within its optimum range of ecological amplitude (Figure 1-13). For example, in alpine regions in Alaska and Norway the lichen *Cladonia alpestris* is dominant and suppresses other lichens, mosses, and even low shrubs when it is growing under optimum conditions; but under less favorable ones it competes poorly. In Alaska *Vaccinium uliginosum* has a moderately wide range of ecological amplitude, but apparently it is dominant only within its optimum range. Species with wide ecological amplitude, such as *Vaccinium vitis-idaea* in Alaska and Norway, and *Agropyron smithii* and *Bouteloua curtipendula* in the Great Plains and adjacent foothills of the Rocky Mountains, occur in many communities, but as dominants they occur only in sites where their competitive capacities can be well developed.

Root systems of plants play a very important part in competition. When the root systems of different species are in the same horizons, competition is often severe for limited supplies of moisture, nitrates, and other resources. *Bromus tectorum,* a winter annual in many parts of the western United States, by its early spring

Figure 1-13. A stand of Ladino clover (*Trifolium repens* var. *Ladino*), showing maximum competitive capacity, is growing here on slightly wet, silty clay soil, well within its range of optimum ecological amplitude. A plentiful supply of readily exchangeable potassium in the soil is needed to enable legumes to compete successfully with grasses. Arkansas. (U.S.D.A. Soil Conservation Service.)

growth and the numerous roots in the surface soil, reduces the moisture to such a degree that slow-growing annuals or perennials are seriously retarded in establishment, growth, or survival. In Idaho only a few seedlings of the shrub *Purshia tridentata* are able to survive the competition of *Bromus tectorum* during the first summer, being better able to compete with broad-leaved summer annuals than with *Bromus*.[110] One reason for the success of crested wheatgrass, smooth bromegrass, and other species that are used in reseeding rangelands, is the rapid development of roots after germination. The top inch or two of soil is likely to dry very soon after a rain, so the seedlings with roots several inches long that penetrate into moist soil have a great advantage in competition over other, shallow-rooted plants.

Geographic location may influence competition, as in southern Idaho where *Agropyron spicatum* and *Artemisia tridentata* compete severely, while in central Washington they seem, instead, to be complementary.[64]

The competitive advantage of one species over another may be caused by greater **cation-exchange capacity** or by greater adaptability in modifying this capacity in relation to the soil. Experiments have shown that plants such as wheat, beans, tomato, and peas vary in capacity to adapt to different concentrations of cations and anions in the soil. The root CEC, operating in accordance with the Donnan equilibrium, is not the only factor governing ion uptake, for plants also differ in the second kind of passive absorption, diffusion; and also in capacity to carry on active absorption against a concentration gradient and the Donnan equilibrium gradients at the expense of respiratory energy.[208]

Seedlings of grasses and forbs encounter great difficulty in becoming established in grasslands that are in good condition, but do so readily in bare areas caused by drought, overgrazing, or other disturbance. The competitive relationships are often intricate, as, for example, in New South Wales, Australia, when seeds of *Bothriochloa ambigua,* a grass of low grazing value, and *Danthonia* spp., with higher grazing value, are both disseminated into a bare area. Here the latter species have only a limited effect on the former, not enough to prevent *Bothriochloa* from becoming established as the dominant. The more vigorous root growth of *Bothriochloa,* as compared to *Danthonia,* gives the former an initial advantage in competition. But in native pastures already occupied by *Danthonia,* invasion by *Bothriochloa* is not likely to occur unless the former have been weakened by overgrazing.[148] Plants propagating vegetatively have an advantage in invading bare areas because the shoots during establishment secure water and nutrients, and possibly also synthesized substances, from the parent plants.

Competition and adaptation have played important roles in the survival of species in various environments, and the space and time in which a species grows are often decisive. Shallow-rooted plants, by rapid growth when soil moisture is adequate, can escape competition with deep-rooted, slow-growing plants. A number of single-stalked grasses, forbs, mosses, and lichens can grow in the large spaces between bunchgrasses but cannot endure the competition in the small spaces between densely growing rhizome grasses. Plants of many species often grow together at the same time in habitats where the environmental resources are ample, but when the resources are limited in quantity or duration, rigorous natural selection of adapted biotypes has occurred. In desert areas of the southwestern United States species of annual life-form are numerous, partly because competition has been reduced by growing in different seasons, e.g., *Streptanthus arizonicus* completes its life-cycle in the cool, late winter while *Amaranthus palmeri* thrives in the warmth of August and September.[178]

Competition between species and strains of forage plants may be severe for soil moisture, nutrients, and light. For example, in an experiment in Iowa the relative capacity of two strains and four species of legumes was determined by growing them in association at the same time, with the result that Madrid sweet clover rated first, followed in order by African alfalfa, Ranger alfalfa, Kenland red clover, and Ladino white clover. The ranking was the same as for relative yields when grown singly, so apparently a close relationship exists between competitive and yielding capacities in this case[186] (Figure 1-14). The competitive ability of one strain or species as compared to that of another may be controlled to some extent by measures such as the application of

Figure 1-14. Competition may be reduced by the association of unlike species as in this artificial community of smooth bromegrass (*Bromus inermis*) and alfalfa (*Medicago sativa*). Competitive capacity of plants is influenced by the intensity of grazing and trampling. July, Lake Geneva, Wisconsin. (U.S.D.A. Soil Conservation Service.)

fertilizer (kind, time, amount) and the intensity and time of mowing or grazing. In Pennsylvania the late removal of the first crop, nitrogen fertilization, and higher levels of mowing increased the growth of smooth bromegrass and orchardgrass but decreased that of Ladino clover.[181]

Moderate grazing by sheep for several seasons eliminates many weedy forbs and as a result the less preferred grasses grow better; on the other hand, heavy grazing by cattle gives some weeds better opportunity to grow. In a careful study of the Wasatch Plateau in Utah, Ellison[77] has shown that the kinds of species in stands heavily grazed by sheep are markedly different from comparable stands that are either not grazed or are grazed by cattle. Competition between legumes and grasses in the seedling stage may be avoided by planting them in alternate drill rows, and this offsets the tendency for grasses to dominate when sowing is done

Figure 1-15. Association of smooth bromegrass and alfalfa apparently benefits both. Density, cover, and vigor are excellent here. Nebraska. (U.S.D.A. Soil Conservation Service.)

in cool, wet weather and for legumes to dominate when warm, dry conditions occur.

Differences of Species in Capacity of Association

This is often called **interspecific association,** and refers to species, mostly in different genera, living together in an area and drawing upon a common pool of resources. Similarity in requirements and ecological amplitude is often essential, especially in habitats characterized by limiting factors such as soil salinity or the shortness of the growing season. In Spitzbergen some species such as *Saxifraga oppositifolia, Cerastium arcticum, Salix polaris, Draba subcapitata, Papaver dahlianum, Phippsia algida,* and *Poa alpina vivipara* meet one of the first requirements for association because they can endure the short growing season at 600 to 800 m above sealevel.[174]

Species of different life-form are often associated because they use the environmental resources at different times or in different spaces. Association results at times because some species require the shade cast by taller plants or the protection from grazing afforded by cacti or thorny shrubs. Nutritional advantages may occur, as in grasses and legumes growing together; for example, both bromegrass and alfalfa, or Ladino clover, benefit when planted for hay or pasture, as is commonly done in the Corn Belt (see Figures 1-14 and 1-15). Bromegrass produces more stems, more growth after cutting, and more seeds because of the nitrogen supplied by the legume, while the protein content of the alfalfa is greater than when it is grown alone, probably because of decreased loss of leaves. Birdsfoot trefoil when grown with grasses shows less lodging and increased yields of seed, but tall orchardgrass and timothy tend to delay its maturity. When grown with Kentucky bluegrass, trefoil's ripening was the same as when grown alone. After the first harvest year, mixtures produced slightly higher yields than the trefoil in single culture.[6] In a seeded *Festuca-Agrostis* grassland reverting to original sward, *Lolium perenne* and *Trifolium repens* were positively associated, but lack of association existed between *Agrostis tenuis* and these two

Figure 1-16. Successful association of longleaf pine (*Pinus palustris*) and carpetgrass (*Axanopus compressus*) is shown in two well-defined layers in the summer aspect. August, Tifton, Georgia. (U. S. Forest Service.)

species and with *Dactylis glomerata,* as well as between *Dactylis* and both *Lolium* and *Trifolium.* The positive correlation may have been caused by a higher nitrogen requirement of *Lolium* which was supplied by *Trifolium.* This correlation tended to disappear as the community became increasingly integrated.[126]

Two or more species may be independently associated, i.e., the various species are able to grow in the environment created by the whole community rather than because of direct interrelations between species; for example, in Norway *Linum catharticum* and *Briza media* grow in calcareous soils, one seldom occurring without the other[79] (Figure 1-16). Positive correlation in the distribution of species in an area may indicate that certain habitats are more suitable for some species than for others, or that one kind makes conditions favorable for the occurrence of others. Many terms used in plant sociology, such as "association" itself, reflect the importance of the subject of interspecific association. Certain groupings in Australia such as *Dodonaea* and *Vittadinia* communities on ridges and *Bassia* and *Cassia* in the valleys, are related to topographic conditions. Other pairs of species showing strong association are *Bassia uniflora-Zygophyllum apiculatum,* and *Cassia eremophila-Westringia rigida.*[93]

Association may favor the establishment of groupings under difficult conditions as, for example, near the central California coast, where trees, by the condensation of atmospheric moisture, provide suitable conditions for the growth of certain orchids and seedlings of Douglas fir, Monterey cypress, and Eucalyptus.[154] In arctic and alpine regions some species become established in the cushions of *Silene acaulis* and *Arenaria obtusiloba.* However, the advantages of association are often not well understood, as in the frequent association of *Diapensia lapponica* and *Vaccinium uliginosum* in Greenland,[18] or *Cassiope tetragona* and *V. uliginosum* in northwestern Alaska.[100]

The causes and processes involved in interspecific association are exceedingly complex. Results secured in the study of animal populations may be helpful; for example, instances of both facilitation and interference have been found among 22 strains of *Drosophila melanogaster* when they were living together as compared to strains living separately, so it appears that the viability of one strain is a function of others coexisting with it.[135] However, in plants the influence is usually less direct than in animals. Trees, for example, may influence the ground vegetation by absorbing nutrients deep in the soil and depositing them by leaf fall on the surface. The effect may be specific, as shown by the luxuriant growth of nettle under alder in Great Britain, while under pines bracken communities develop, and under larch the bramble is dominant.[158]

Excretions and products of decomposition, by preventing the growth of some species and favoring that of others, may influence the formation or maintenance of certain plant groupings. Substances such as biotin, thiamine, vitamin B_{12}, histidine, and uracil may be stimulative or even essential for some species. Inhibitory substances include penicillin produced by *Penicillium notatum,* glytoxin by the soil fungus *Glocladium,* absinthin by *Artemisia absinthium,* 3-acetyl-6-methoxy-benzaldehyde by the desert plant *Encelia farinosa,* juglone by *Juglans nigra,* and cinnamic acid by *Parthenium argentatum.*[19,20] Species of sunflower differ in their sensitivity to toxins given off by grasses, which affect the association of these species according to the kinds and concentrations of the toxins and the tolerances of various kinds of sunflowers.[4] It appears also that alkaloids, leached from leaves or roots, may have important ecological influences.[149]

Although many details regarding interactions are not well understood, it is clear that the requirements of species or ecotypes and their ecological amplitudes play essential roles in independent association and in positive and negative correlation in the distribution of species.

Differences of Species in Reproductive Processes

The adaptability of plants for pollination; the production, dispersal, and germination of seeds; and vegetative propagation are considered in this section. Wind-pollinated plants depend for success upon the production of large quantities of pollen, while insect-pollinated ones depend upon special structures, colors, or fragrance. Important factors in pollination include the quantity and viability of pollen produced, distance the pollen is carried, length of time during which production and dispersal occurs, and the distance between individuals in a population. In Nebraska, for example, smooth bromegrass produces more pollen than crested and intermediate wheatgrasses and switchgrass, and most of the pollen is dispersed within 5 to 15 rods. The average period of dispersal per inflorescence varies from 8 days in crested wheatgrass to 12 days in switchgrass.[119] In eastern Colorado, Russian wildrye (*Elymus junceus*) sheds pollen mostly between 4 and 5 P. M. throughout a 9-day period at the end of May and early June. The shedding is very sensitive to temperature, which varies considerably at this time, and this may explain in part why the seed production is erratic in this region.[70A] Apparently grasses are usually pollinated by nearby plants, for example, orchardgrass averaged 62.4 seeds per panicle when the pollinating plants were within 1.5 yd of one another, but only 27.2 seeds per panicle at greater distances up to 11.5 yd.[96]

Although strong winds and air currents carry many kinds of pollen to great heights and distances,[210] it is questionable how much pollination is accomplished in this way. The pollen of pines appears to be dispersed as much as 100 miles, but the amount is limited; of cotton, up to 4200 ft; and of corn, occasionally to 400 ft. The great frequency of natural hybrids in grasses is brought about by the association of many individuals of different species, the large production of wind-borne pollen, and the similarity in reproductive organs of different species.[183] Separation of wind-pollinated plants such as pines and oaks by a few miles may not prevent cross-pollination, but in insect-pollinated trees a few hundred yards may be very effective.[109] Insect-pollination from a distance, however, may not be entirely prevented, because numerous insects of various species are in the air on warm days to heights of several thousand feet.[115] Plants and animals possess many adaptations that facilitate cross-pollination or prevent self-pollination.

Dispersal of seeds and spores is accomplished in many well-known ways but concrete data on distances they are carried are scarce. Most seeds seem rarely to be dispersed beyond 300 ft, the greatest distance winged seeds and fruits are carried is about 880 yd, but dust seeds and plumed fruits may be carried as much

Figure 1-17. Rapid growth with only slight competition of seedlings produced this stand of annual meadow barley (*Hordeum brachyantherum*) in a moist gully bottom, but run-off from a high-intensity storm could wash all the plants away. Utah. (U. S. Forest Service.)

as 700 miles.[172] Only one example will be cited: the rough, reticulate coats of the minute seeds of tobacco (*Nicotiana* spp.) appear to be an outstanding adaptation to the invasion of disturbed sites, which are the most common habitats of many species in this genus.[202]

Barriers such as mountain ranges or adverse climatic conditions are important in forming limits to the distribution of species, and therefore some plants are not found in habitats that would be suitable, but succeed when introduced artificially, e.g., European weeds introduced into the United States, and vice versa. The dispersal capacity of a species may be overrated, for there is no real evidence that plants possessing specialized mechanisms are more widely distributed than those without them.[92] In a limited area without important barriers, however, dispersal tends to maintain the several stands of a community-type uniform in composition. Because of the effectiveness of dispersal of all sorts of propagules, unoccupied habitats suitable for a given species will soon be reached by individuals of that species, with the result that similar habitats in a restricted area will be occupied by similar groupings of plants and animals.[70]

Plants with seeds varying in period of dormancy have advantages in surviving unfavorable conditions. Retention of viability for several years appears advantageous to plants such as *Minuartia stricta* which have little competitive capacity,[163] to many legumes, and others. Some seeds of annuals lie dormant in the soil in grasslands for a number of years before bare areas appear. Seedlings in such spots are likely to survive but those that appear among other plants usually die. Annual species are often dependent for dispersal and survival upon large supplies of seeds and high rates of germination; and low production may restrict the distribution of a species, as in northwestern Montana where one of the factors in maintaining a stable ecotone of aspen woodland and grassland has been stated to be the poor seed crops of the former, caused probably by unfavorable climatic conditions.[138] The restricted distribution in the Sahara and Negev of the shrub *Calligonum comosum* to coarse sandy soils where the rainfall is low, is probably because this substratum provides conditions needed for germination, as it is known that the seeds fail to germinate in the light, at high temperatures, or even in close contact with water.[128]

Figure 1-18. *Aster foliaceous* is capable of invading eroded depressions by means of rhizomes, but seedlings would have difficulty. A few plants of *Geranium, Eriogonum, Achillea,* and *Vicia* are intermixed here. Steel tape shows former soil level. August, 10,000 ft, Utah. (U. S. Forest Service.)

A number of species have pronounced capacity to form new stands following fire or other disturbance (Figures 1-17 and 1-18); for example, seeds may be protected within cones as in the lodgepole pine (*Pinus contorta* ssp. *murrayana*), or they may have great mobility as in the fireweed (*Epilobium angustifolium*). The crowns or rhizomes may survive fire and produce new shoots, e.g., *Populus tremuloides, Salix pulchra,* many grasses, and some plants of *Purshia tridentata.* The mobility and high viability of many seeds enable some species to form pioneer communities such as *Populus sargentii, Salix nigra,* and *S. interior* on sandbars, Russian thistle (*Salsola kali*) and other weeds in abandoned fields, *Betula populifolia* in devastated forests, and *Rubus occidentalis* in burned-over forests (Figures 1-17 and 1-18).

Birds are important in dispersing seeds. Certain cereals and weeds grow on the feeding grounds of gulls,[84] and in Norway the tits (*Farus* spp., *Sitta europaea*) contribute to the dispersal of *Galeopsis tetrahit, G. bifida,* and *Juniperus communis* by gathering and storing seeds.[97] The rarity of *Mercurialis perennis* in Ireland, in spite of having been widely introduced, is evidently the result of the absence or extreme infrequency of any agent of dispersal. This species does not lack genetic variability nor is there lack of suitable habitats. In Britain, where certain kinds of mice and ants occur which may be the agents of transport, the plant is aggressive and common.[17]

Under severe conditions where production of seed is hazardous, vivipary and other forms of apomixis may be advantageous. **Vivipary,** or the formation of vegetative buds in place of florets, is frequent in the grass family, for example, in *Poa bulbosa* and *Festuca vivipara.* Apomixis and self-pollination may result in the formation and perpetuation of single biotypes, so that the population has a high degree of genetic homogeneity, well adapted to a particular habitat, but even in such a population differences in microhabitat conditions and competition will induce phenotypic variations among the individuals.

If the biotype possesses a high degree of adaptability it can live in a variety of microhabitats and survive unfavorable conditions better than if it possesses less. The greater the number of biotypes

Figure 1-19. Vigorous propagation of black gramagrass (*Bouteloua eriopoda*), by stolons is characteristic of this important range grass in southern New Mexico. (U. S. Forest Service.)

in a population, the greater will be the genetic diversity and adaptability of the population, and hence the survival under unfavorable conditions. This greater adaptability in growth-form, earliness of growth and maturity, size of seed, and resistance to disease are important in determining the extent of the geographic distribution of a species; the decumbent, rhizomatous growth-form of *Panicum virgatum,* for example, is more common in sandy soils in northern and western Nebraska, while the erect, bunch type is more common in southeastern Nebraska.[73]

The Mendelian population, consisting of cross-pollinating individuals, is a more plastic system of adaptability than an asexual array of organisms. Species equipped with both sexual and asexual kinds of reproduction have distinct advantages over those that have only one, because the former are able to maintain the same genotype almost indefinitely in propagating biotypes, and at the same time they benefit from the formation of new genotypes in sexual reproduction (Figure 1-19). A striking example of this is found in the genus *Rubus,* in which a complicated polymorphism and great adaptability have led to widespread distribution in Australia and other countries.[108] Vegetative propagation is of great value to many species not only in maintaining the population under conditions adverse for seed production, but also in enabling it to invade adjacent areas.

Limitation of pollination and dispersal in a small area may promote the formation of new ecotypes. This appears to follow from the conclusion of Ford [80] that when a population is subdivided into small isolated, or partly isolated, units rapid evolution is favored because each group can then become adjusted to the particular habitat conditions instead of to the average conditions over a large area. Similar conditions obtain in marginal populations within the area of distribution of a species, for such populations may possess less heterozygosis than those in the central part of the range of distribution.[30] A high degree of heterozygosis often gives the population greater plasticity, and in many cases leads to greater capacity to cope with variations in the environment.[145]

The number of individuals in a population, accompanied by heightened variability, increases during favorable environmental periods. This greater intensity of variability permits genes to be combined in new ways, and some of the resulting combinations may give increased adaptability during less favorable environmental periods or in relationships with other organisms. Disturbance of natural conditions by man, or the formation of new habitats by natural causes such as erosion, recession of glaciers, or emergence from water, may provide suitable habitats for hybrid populations. As suggested by Anderson,[3] the habitat needs "hybridizing" before hybrids can survive, e.g., irises or oaks,[108] for in the undisturbed habitat they are unable to compete with individuals of the parent genotypes. Populations of different species may be sufficiently close to one another geographically (sympatric) so that ecologically successful hybrids are formed, followed by introgressive hybridization, as in the case of *Quercus velutina,* for example, which has been enriched by characters from *Q. borealis* in the Great Smoky Mountains.[206] In the Canary Islands *Pinus canariensis* forest forms an ecological pathway connecting the subalpine scrub with the laurel forest below, so that populations of *Adenocarpus* spp. come into contact with one another and hybridize successfully. The populations are highly variable, especially in the lower pine forest, and hybrids are able to survive on burned-over areas. These hybrids are often associated with *Cistus monspeliensis,* a good fire indicator.[134] The crossing of two formerly geographically separated species (allopatric) may result in a highly competitive hybrid where a suitable habitat occurs; for example, the fertile *Spartina townsendii* ($2n = 126$), in Southampton Water, England, is a hybrid of *S. maritima* ($2n = 56$) and the North American *S. alterniflora* ($2n = 70$).[109] In this way hybridization and introgression may cause the submergence of small isolated populations.

Differences of Species in Resistance to Grazing, Mowing, or Other Treatment

This fourth group of disjunctive interrelationships between plants and other organisms includes the feeding on many plants by many kinds of animals, from nematodes and slugs to cattle, trampling by larger animals, and clipping or mowing by various animals and man. Because of the long period of adaptation of grassland species in the Great Plains to both adverse physical conditions and grazing, the resulting grassland types are some of the most durable of any found today. Stands comprising such species as *Agropyron smithii, Stipa comata, Bouteloua gracilis,* and *Carex filifolia* are capable of enduring prolonged drought, severe infestations of grasshoppers, and much overgrazing. In the arctic tundra perennial herbs possess great capacity to recover from grazing throughout the year by lemming, even though the growing season of the plants lasts only seven to ten weeks.[164]

Grasses, especially those with rhizomes or runners, withstand grazing, trampling, or mowing better than forbs. The latter, having growing points above the surface of the ground, are usually more susceptible to damage from these causes as well as from desiccation and freezing than the former, with less exposed growing points. Excessive plant growth in some species such as perennial ryegrass, unless it is moderately grazed or mowed, may result in elevated crowns, inhibition of tillering, and greater suscept-

Figure 1-20. An ungrazed stand of Idaho fescue (*Festuca idahoensis*), a bunchgrass highly relished by cattle. (Cf. Figure 1-21.) Note sharp transitions between vegetation types. Northeastern California. (U. S. Forest Service.)

ibility to frost damage. The various biotypes and ecotypes within a grass species usually vary considerably even in the same region, so strains desired for grazing or for mowing can usually be readily developed in breeding programs.

Each kind of animal has preferences for certain kinds of plants (Figures 1-20 and 1-21). Some feed on a variety of species, others on only a few, or on only one. Sheep as a rule choose broad-leaved herbs (forbs) and the tender parts of grasses, cattle and horses usually prefer grasses, and deer and moose browse on many kinds of shrubs and trees. These preferences are caused partly by the requirements and habits of the animals and partly by the palatability or desirability of the plants. Differences in palatability occur between strains of grasses as well as between species, and are caused by variations in succulence, food content (sugar, protein, starch, fat, vitamin A), fiber and ash contents, presence of volatile oils, disease incidence, and stage of maturity. Relative proportion of species in the stand, familiarity of the animal with

Figure 1-21. Cattle have selected Idaho fescue, resulting in the death of many bunches, thus giving opportunity for the invasion of less palatable species. (Cf. Figure 1-20.) Northeastern California. (U. S. Forest Service.)

Figure 1-22. Protected from grazing, mountain brome-grass is maintaining itself in competition with coneflower (*Rudbeckia occidentalis*). Note clumping of vigorous aspens. (Cf. Fig. 1-22A.) Aug., Manti-La Sal Natl. Forest, Utah. (U. S. Forest Service.)

the plant, degree of hunger or desire of the animal for a particular kind of plant, and the availability of the plant are also influencing factors.

Under close grazing a cow or sheep may graze poisonous plants which remain untouched under moderate grazing. A very palatable species may be eliminated from a stand because of severe grazing and may not be able to re-establish itself, thus less palatable plants are given opportunity to invade; for example, the replacement of grasses by annual weeds in prairie dog towns, and by buffalograss in the northern Great Plains and mesquite in the semidesert grassland in the Southwest. Heavy grazing has favored the spread of poisonous plants on wide areas of western range lands (Figures 1-22 and 1-22A). Overgrazing may reduce competition to such an extent that species near the limits of their geographic ranges can become dominant, as where buffalograss replaces taller grasses in the northern Great Plains.

Intensive grazing not only reduces the competitive capacity of

Figure 1-22A. Under grazing, *Rudbeckia occidentalis* has almost replaced the palatable mountain brome-grass. Spruce trees invading aspen grove in background. (Cf. Fig. 1-22.) Aug., Manti-La Sal Natl. Forest, Utah. (U. S. Forest Service.)

preferred species and the interspecific association of many species, but may also damage some of the most favorable habitats. Excessive trampling of nonsandy soils causes packing, and reduces the accumulation of mulch and organic matter and the infiltration of water. Droppings and liquid manure may also modify the soil and, where they are excessive, permit invasion of certain weeds. Reduction in height and density of the vegetation increases soil temperature and evaporation rate, so that the changed habitat conditions may no longer be within the ranges of ecological amplitudes of preferred species. Severe overgrazing in the Wasatch Plateau in Utah has resulted in eroded habitats and displacement of herbs and shrubs by an open stand of species such as *Festuca ovina, Poa* spp., and *Sedum stenopetalum,* capable of growing on erosion pavement.[77] It appears, therefore, that plants have a high degree of specificity for various durations and intensities of overgrazing. This specificity is also present in various stages of succession on abandoned farmlands. In Idaho, for example, populations of Russian thistle, mustards, and downy bromegrass have optimal time and space requirements for their appearance.[162]

Preferred species that grow sparsely are most susceptible to elimination by overgrazing, for they are closely grazed while less palatable and more abundant kinds remain untouched. In the Front Range in central Colorado, bunches of grasses such as *Muhlenbergia montana* under close grazing tend to break into small parts, becoming sod-like, while other grasses such as *Festuca arizonica* are more resistant to disintegration. However, in both, plant vigor is reduced and *Bouteloua gracilis* replaces them, while forage yields decrease.[118] Heavy grazing may also cause clumps of the last-mentioned grass to separate into smaller, closer-spaced tufts, and bunches of *Stipa comata* to become smaller and more decumbent, with fewer stems and finer, shorter leaves. The capacity of grasses to endure grazing is related to characteristics such as a decumbent growth-form, rhizome production, large food reserves, rapid growth renewal and production of new shoots, long season of vegetative growth, location of growth-renewal tissue below the lowest level of grazing, and resistance to unfavorable environmental conditions, especially drought.

Selection plays an important role in the development of ecotypes suited to different conditions. For example, stands of perennial ryegrass, Kentucky bluegrass, and orchardgrass, have been grown for many years, especially in England, under various treatments such as grazed or ungrazed, mowed or unmowed, and, in addition, in moist or dry soils with high or low fertility. Grazed pastures have produced ecotypes that are earlier in maturity and more decumbent than meadows, with the result that the latter tend to disappear when subjected to grazing, while pasture types disappear under mowing. In this process of becoming adapted to specific habitats the ecological amplitude of the population becomes narrower, at least for some conditions.

Alteration of the habitat may thus bring about the survival of certain biotypes and in time the formation of ecotypes, and the loss of other biotypes. Man can, by various management operations such as controlling the intensity and time of grazing or mowing, application of fertilizers, or the soil-water content by irrigation or drainage, exercise considerable influence on the evolutionary process. These manipulations change the environmental conditions so that the requirements of some species or ecotypes are secured more readily, and consequently they become more vigorous and stronger competitors, while other ecotypes may not be able to grow at all because their ranges of ecological amplitude have been surpassed. The management of one or more environmental conditions may be of greater importance in certain places than the course of nature in determining the success or failure of species, particularly in the central European grasslands.[75,76] Success in management operations depends upon knowledge of the requirements and ecological amplitudes of species and ecotypes.

Grasses have considerable capacity to survive the combined effects of drought and grasshopper infestations which occur frequently in the Great Plains (Figure 1-23). Most species of grasshoppers show selectivity, some feeding only on grasses, some only on forbs or shrubs, and others on both grasses and broad-leaved plants; in Montana, for example, certain species feed mainly on *Bouteloua gracilis,* others on *Agropyron smithii* or *Stipa comata.* The

Figure 1-23. Grasses in the Great Plains have become adapted to endure the effects of prolonged drought and grasshopper infestations. Grass stalks, cut off by grasshoppers, have been washed up against low shrubs by recent rains. August, 1936, western North Dakota.

height, density, growth-form, and succulence of plants influence the selectivity, consequently different species of plants are affected according to the kinds and abundance of grasshoppers that are present in an area. *Agropyron smithii* may be seriously attacked in some years and places while other species are much less affected. Weedy grasses, including *Schedonnardus paniculatus, Munroa squarrosa,* and *Bromus tectorum,* are attacked by fewer kinds than the important forage species named above.[50] The requirements of grasshoppers and locusts often vary according to the stage of the life-cycle, as has been shown in East Africa, where the requirements of nymphs, fledglings, young adults, and egg-laying adults of the red locust are found in mesic vegetation, in which low grass, tall grass, and bare soil alternate—the characteristic mosaic found in all outbreak areas.[9]

In contrast to the feeding habits of many grasshoppers, weedy

Figure 1-24. A grove of chestnut (*Castanea dentata*) in Virginia before the blight struck. (U. S. Forest Service.)

Figure 1-24A. Chestnut trees killed or injured by the blight (*Endothia parasitica*). Photograph taken in 1928, in Maryland. (U. S. Forest Service.)

Figure 1-24B. A mixed stand of ash, red oak, and red hickory replacing dead chestnuts killed by blight in 1916. Photograph taken in 1940, in Maryland. (U. S. Forest Service.)

species of plants may be preferred by some kinds of insects. The beet leafhopper, which transmits curly top virus disease to sugar beets and other crops, prefers weeds, particularly Russian thistle and mustards on recently abandoned fields and overgrazed ranges in the western United States. Plants in the later stages of succession, such as *Bromus tectorum* and the perennials, are not suitable hosts. Thus the destruction of the first weed invaders by this insect may hasten the establishment and growth of the more permanent species.[162]

Differences of Species in Susceptibility to Parasites

Differences between species may be caused by the resistance capacity of the host, the degree of virulence and abundance of the parasite, and by environmental conditions. The chestnut blight is an outstanding example of a high degree of virulence of a parasite in a nonresistant host, resulting in the virtual elimination of the chestnut from the deciduous forests of eastern North America (Figures 1-24, 1-24A, 1-24B).

The most widespread pathogens in grasses, especially rusts, attack leaves. Other important diseases are root and crown rots, head and leaf smuts, ergots, and other seed disorders.[98] Variation between strains in resistance to pathogens is one of the criteria for the selection of plants for cultivation and breeding; for example, the susceptibility of the Merion strain of Kentucky bluegrass to stripe smut (*Ustilago striiformis*) is much greater than that of other varieties and selections.[129] Common insect parasites on grasses are the spittlebug in humid regions, mites in the Pacific Northwest, and thrips, chinch bugs, grasshoppers, and white grubs in various areas.[98]

Effects of parasites include the reduction of vigor and consequent loss of competitive capacity, decreased range of ecological amplitude, loss in capacity to use the resources of the environment, and decreased yields of herbage and seed. The association of species and management practice may influence the degree of parasitism; for example, the spread of crown gall was less rapid on alfalfa when grown in association with smooth bromegrass than when it was grown alone.[36] Blind seed disease on ryegrass in Oregon can be effectively controlled by deep and early plow-

Figure 1-25. An example of commensalism—rootless Spanish moss (*Tillandsia usneoides*) attached to an old live oak (*Quercus virginiana*). Brackish marsh is shown in the background. Spanish moss has a wide distribution, from southern Maryland through tropical America to Argentina and Chile. February, Louisiana. (U.S.D.A. Soil Conservation Service.)

ing, stubble burning, seed inspection, and other agronomic measures.[107] Dallisgrass, an important forage plant in Georgia, dies when it is not mowed, evidently because of foliage diseases; but vaseygrass, on the other hand, soon dies when it is mowed or grazed too closely.[98]

Several examples of the effects of parasites on the grouping of species will be given. The wood-rotting fungus *Fomes ignarius*, wood-boring larvae of the beetle *Saperda*, and the defoliating beetle *Phytodecta americana* place the aspen at a disadvantage in competing with grasses at the ecotones between grassland and aspen groveland in northwestern Montana.[138] In moist years in Kansas, as in 1940 to 1942, the prickly-pear cactus is so heavily infested with insects that it may disappear from some communities, while in dry years it tends to increase.[193] And in Hawaii, the introduced *Procedidochares utilis,* a tetritid gall fly, has eliminated the weed *Eupatorium adenophorum* from some large areas, but has had little effect in other places.[12] The selectivity of parasites, as exemplified by this gall fly, is of major importance in the biological control of weeds.

Differences of Species in Mutualistic and Commensal Relations

In **mutualistic relations** both of the associated organisms presumably benefit. Nitrogen-fixation bacteria are most commonly associated with legumes, but they are also found with alders and the black locust, which may owe their special capacity to invade bare areas to these bacteria in their root nodules, thus hastening plant succession by supplying needed nitrogen. In **commensal relations,** such as lichens and mosses growing on the bark of trees, one of the plants benefits while the other may be injured very slightly, or not at all (Figure 1-25).

The association of a fungus with a root is known as **mycorrhiza.** When the fungus is present inside the cells the association is **endotrophic,** occurring characteristically in the Ericaceae and Orchidaceae, and also in grasses and other plants. When the fungus is growing on the surface of the root, as is common in woody plants such as pines, spruces, beeches, oaks, aspens, and hazels, the association is **ectotrophic.** Mycorrhizae are usually considered a kind of mutualism in which the fungus appears to absorb carbohydrates and possibly other organic substances from the root, while the latter presumably obtains nitrogen and minerals from the fungus. It appears that the fungus, in addition to absorbing nitrogen compounds from the soil, can in some instances fix atmospheric nitrogen. Some kinds of mutualism such as ectotrophic mycorrhiza may be the most successful type of parasitism because there is no destruction of tissue, although hypertrophy may be induced. Other kinds of parasitism are "primitive," in which the parasites are restricted by the host, although seedlings may be destroyed; "less primitive," when the parasites are less restricted and cause rapid and widespread destruction of the host tissues; and "specialized," in which some degree of temporary mutualism occurs and disorganization of host tissue is reduced or delayed.[50]

Mutualistic relations may be of great advantage to plants, for without the special absorbing capacity of the fungi, or the nutritive features of associated bacteria, they might not be able to utilize the resources of the environment adequately. If both associates are present, otherwise uninhabitable sites may be occupied, but there may be delay in invasion because two different organisms must migrate into the new area and come together. However, the advantages of mutualistic relations seem to outweigh the disadvantages, as indicated by their widespread occurrence.

ECOLOGICAL SUCCESS OF A SPECIES

The ecological success of a species or a population depends upon its capacity to cope with its physical environment and with the associated plants and animals in the relationships outlined in the preceding principles. This capacity has been attained over a long period of evolution during which the fitness of adaptations to the physical environment and to interspecific association became increasingly close. The adaptiveness is generally so efficient that new migrants or hybrids and mutants can find opportunity to grow only in disturbed areas where the original vegetation has been destroyed or impaired. It appears that every species has its ecological niche and that most niches are fully occupied until disturbed.

The degree of success of an individual organism depends upon how well its processes are integrated with the environment and with other organisms and how well it functions as a member of the species population. Similarly, the success of a population depends upon the integration of population processes and relationships with other species populations and with the environment.

The processes involved in attaining ecological success are very different for a plant growing alone or in a spaced planting such as a corn field, where the relations are chiefly with the physical environment, than for a plant growing in a dense vegetation composed of many species, as in a meadow. The ecological success of a species may be measured or described according to quantitative and qualitative characteristics of the community, such as numerical abundance, cover, frequency, vitality, and other features, as discussed in Chapter 2.

The perennial bunchgrass, little bluestem (*Andropogon scoparius*), may be taken as an example of a highly successful species, judging by its wide distribution, abundance or dominance, and per-

Figure 1-26. The perennial bunchgrass, little bluestem (*Andropogon scoparius*), is a highly successful species. Here it is shown growing in excellent condition on stony soil in Texas. (U.S.D.A. Soil Conservation Service.)

sistence. Its requirements of water and mineral nutrients can be secured in moist to fairly dry soil, ranging from loam to soil of a sandy or rocky texture. Thus little bluestem has a wide range of ecological amplitude in respect to soil fertility and moisture, as well as duration of light and length of growing season, but it does not tolerate much shade. A number of ecotypes are known, and probably many more exist (Figure 1-26). Its numerous leaves and extensive fibrous root system make it efficient in photosynthesis and absorption of water, so it has a well-developed capacity for using the resources of the environment, as well as for competing with other plants except where it is overtopped. However, in very dry habitats such as the High Plains of Colorado, it cannot compete with the lower-growing shortgrasses. Although occurring usually as a dominant, its bunch life-form permits other species to grow in association with it. Flowers are produced on stalks 50 to 150 cm tall, so they are well exposed to pollination by wind, and the fruits are adapted to wind dissemination although they may also be carried by animals. Large yields of seed, maturing in late summer or early fall, are dependent upon suitable temperatures and moisture supply during blooming and later, but such conditions do not obtain every year. The seed is dormant for two to four months after maturity, germination is slow, and the small seedlings grow slowly. Little bluestem tolerates grazing well unless cropped too closely, and it also withstands burning during the nongrowing season. Usually it is not attacked seriously by parasites. The stages encountering greatest hazards for success are those of seed production and seedling establishment.

The capacity to occupy special habitats and the persistence of these habitats are important in the ecological success of many species (Figure 1-27). The requirements and amplitudes of such species have become so well adapted that they cannot compete well elsewhere, but in their own habitats they often have so much competitive capacity that other species cannot usually invade. Species in some communities characterized by *Ammophila, Cakile, Salicornia,* and *Spartina,* have been closely associated on exposed, as well as on protected seashores of the North Atlantic since the Miocene Epoch.[49] Certain parts of northern Alaska and Scandinavia were not glaciated during the Pleistocene, so there has

Figure 1-27. The Washingtonia palm (*Washingtonia fili-fera*) is ecologically successful in limited areas of south-eastern California, Yuma County, Arizona, and in northern Lower California by growing in rocky stream beds or in the vicinity of springs. Near Palm Springs, California. (U. S. Forest Service.)

been a long time for adaptation of plants to special habitats. The roots of a number of species, including *Arctagrostis latifolia* and *Eriophorum vaginatum* var. *spissum,* are able to follow, within about 1 cm, the melting of the permafrost; thus essential rapid growth at low temperatures takes place during the short growing season. The occurrence of certain rare species, such as *Minuartia stricta* and its associates in the North Pennines of Great Britain, is possible because of the maintenance of favorable habitats since the Late-glacial Period.[163]

High-alpine species often seem to be restricted to the high altitudes partly through lack of competitive capacity. They can hold their own only where the usual growth requirements can be met and where the growing season is so short that all plants with longer growing periods and greater competitive capacity, are eliminated. For example, in Swedish Lapland many alpine species, including *Ranunculus nivalis, Salix herbacea, S. polaris, Sibbaldia procumbens,* and *Saxifraga* spp., are found at lower elevations in the conifer and birch zones in certain places such as river banks, inundated lake shores, talus slopes, paths, and old reindeer pens (*Phippsia algida* in the last), where the environmental requirements of alpine plants, including nonpodsolized, nutrient-rich soil and exposure to sunlight, can be supplied, and competition with subalpine plants is reduced or absent.[177] Therefore it appears that the ecological success of alpine plants is attained by their efficiency in using the resources of their environment in a short growing period and in the absence of competition with other species.

In the reseeding of range lands, in the introduction of new crops into a region, and in biological control it is important to evaluate the opportunities for ecological success of ecotypes, varieties, and species that may be used. This includes consideration of their characteristics, particularly the requirements, ecological amplitude, and competitive capacity. The use of the homoclime technique[152] is also helpful in the introduction of new species because it stresses the selection of plants or animals from areas of similar environmental conditions. It has been shown that when a strain grows well in one place, such as in a certain area of California, it will be successful in other areas that are similar in latitude and climate such as parts of Israel, provided that diseases, parasites, or competition are not limiting factors. In order to reduce competition it may be necessary to destroy most of the dominant plants in an area before introducing a species from another region.

GENERAL REFERENCES

Billings, W. D., "The Environmental Complex in Relation to Plant Growth and Distribution," *Quart. Rev. Biol.,* **27**, 251–264 (1952).

Daubenmire, R. F., "Plants and Environment, a Textbook of Plant Autecology," 2nd Ed., John Wiley & Sons, Inc., New York, N.Y., 1959.

Dice, L. R., "Natural Communities," Univ. Michigan Press, Ann Arbor, Mich., 1952.

Heslop-Harrison, J., "New Concepts in Flowering-plant Taxonomy," Harvard Univ. Press, Cambridge, Mass., 1956.

McDougall, W. B., "Plant Ecology," 4th Ed., Lea & Febiger, Philadelphia, Pa., 1949.

GROUPING OF SPECIES

Plants rarely grow singly. Different kinds usually grow together, forming groups such as a patch of weeds on waste-land, a zone of sedges and grasses bordering a lake, or a group of trees forming a woods. Groupings or communities of plants are so universal that they require careful description and study.

A plant grouping is a collection of plants of one to many species growing together and having a certain unity. This unity is formed in the first place because the plants are living close together in a common habitat; and it increases by the interrelationships formed between them. In the more complex communities, composed of plants of various life-forms, interrelationships become more numerous and diversified. Interspecific association of species becomes more pronounced, and thus the dependence of one species upon another within the general framework of the environment increases as well.[189] The independence of a species may be greatly modified when it is growing in association with other species as compared to growing alone.

The extent of the area occupied by each kind of grouping depends chiefly upon the similarity or homogeneity of the environmental conditions (see Figures 1-1 and 1-22). "As widely in space as a uniform physical environment and a uniform physiological interference [similar to relations between species] are maintained, just so widely will the vegetation remain similarly uniform, modified only by the factor of time, which is necessary to the attainment of uniformity." [89,p.446] "Uniformity, area, boundary, and duration are the essentials of a plant community. . . . A community is uniform, either in space or in time, only to a reasonable degree. This uniformity is sufficient to enable us to recognize the community and to accept it as a unit of vegetation. . . ." [90,pp.103,104]

The grouping cannot be separated functionally from the environment. The community with all its plants and animals forms the living part of the ecosystem, while the environment forms the nonliving part. In most ecosystems the kinds of organisms are numerous and diverse and include **producers, consumers,** and **decomposers.** The relations between the organisms themselves, and between the organisms and the environment are also numerous and complex. Because of this complexity and the basic function of plants as producers, and also because they usually form the structural habitat within which animals live, plant groupings are treated primarily here, even though they form only one part of the living component of the ecosystem. The plant grouping is an advantageous starting point because it is more easily analyzed than the animal life or the environment; moreover, an understanding of the plant community facilitates analysis of the other components of the ecosystem. Many plant-animal relations are, of course, included in the study of plant communities, but less exhaustively than when the ecosystem is the primary object of study.

FACTORS INVOLVED IN THE GROUPING OF SPECIES

Groupings of plants occur because the requirements and ecological amplitudes of several to many species are adapted to the environmental conditions of a specific habitat and because the relations between these species permit them to be associated (see Charts 1 and 2, pp. 18 and 19). In other words, the plants and animals in the grouping are able to coexist in the environment of the habitat. In addition, the evolutionary history of the associated species, the environments of the past, and the relict populations of earlier stages of succession influence the association. Plant groupings are not merely random aggregations resulting from the first seeds or other propagules reaching an area. The environmental conditions play a most important role in determining the kinds of plants that become associated. For example, the occurrence of each species in each stage of succession in southern New Mexico[34] and groupings within the extensive grassland of California[15] appear to be determined by the kind of soil in the various areas. Pronounced relationships have been found between the grouping of plants and the soil characteristics in many places[25] as, for example, on well-drained soils in the arctic tundra of northern Alaska, where the correspondence is so close that the vegetation type can be predicted when the soil profile and general location on the Arctic slope are known.[191] In many communities it appears that a state of interaction and coordination between species and the physical environment is gradually produced.[2] This takes a long time, involving the genetic continuity of species. Invaders cannot intrude, for the community develops a characteristic environment which determines the kinds of plants that can grow there.

Some groups contain many species, others few. The number depends largely upon (1) the nature of the habitat, including the length of growing season, availability of moisture and mineral nutrients, and absence of disturbing influences; (2) the degree of overlapping in ranges of ecological amplitude of the species; and (3) sufficient associative capacity so species can live together (see Figures 1-7, 1-17, and 1-27). Each species has its own individuality, but when it becomes a member of a group it is no longer independent—there are too many interacting organisms. The invasion of many plants is often restricted by the strong competitive capacity of various dominant grasses or other plants so that the total number of species may be low—*Agropyron* spp. and *Festuca ovina* var. *duriuscula,* for example, in northeastern Washington.[82]

The interrelations between individuals of the same species may be very close. Natural grafting of roots is common in many kinds of forest-tree species; for example, in the eastern white pine (*Pinus strobus*) from two to a number of trees may become united in this manner.[94] This interaction has pronounced effects upon the nature of the grouping, for the individuality of the single organism is replaced by a complex organism—an interacting group of plants that have many connected physiological processes. Hence, intraspecific competition becomes less important than interspecific competition, and diseases such as Dutch elm disease (*Ceratostomella ulmi*) and oak wilt (*Endoconidiophora fagacearum*) can be transmitted through such grafts from tree to tree. Tree poisons (silvicides) can also move from poisoned to nonpoisoned trees ("backflash"). The disease or the poison transmitted in this way may hasten the death of many desirable trees.

A species with wide ecological amplitude and strong competitive capacity may occur in several different groups. It may be dominant in one group and subordinate in another; for example, in certain clay soils in the northern Great Plains, western wheatgrass (*Agropyron smithii*) is often the chief dominant, while in loam soils it may be present but subordinate to needle-and-thread (*Stipa comata*) and blue gramagrass (*Bouteloua gracilis*). Species may vary in adaptability to different concentrations of mineral salts. As shown in Table 1-1, *Pinus silvestris* has a wide range of amplitude, but it is dominant only when the ground-water level is 30 to 40 cm or more deep. As shown in the table, similarity in amplitudes permits grouping of species into marsh, transition bog, and sphagnum bog.

Largely on the basis of tolerance to depth and duration of snow cover, alpine species may often be differentially aggregated into definite communities. For example, in the Rondane region in Norway there are four communities: *Cetraria nivalis-Alectoria ochroleuca* lichens on exposed ridges, *Cladonia alpestris* lichens on the slope, *Vaccinium myrtillus* heath zone still lower on the slope, and *Deschampsia flexuosa-Carex bigelowii* grassland with a ground layer

Figure 2-1. *Cladonia sylvatica* and *C. alpestris* form most of the lichen layer in openings between the glandular birch (*Betula glandulosa*), while *C. rangiferina* is most abundant under the shrubs. Very good winter caribou range east of Cantwell, Alaska, August, 1957.

of mosses in the bottom of the depression[62] (see Chart 1). Important associates in the first community are *Vaccinium vitis-idaea, Cornicularia divergens,* and *Cetraria cucullata.* Species with wide ecological amplitude such as *Cetraria islandica* and *Dicranum fuscescens* were found in several communities but may be dominant in only one, or at times in none. Competition also plays an important part in the aggregation of the species; for example, where *Cladonia alpestris* forms dense mats there is little opportunity for the growth of less competitive lichens, mosses, and even low shrubs and herbs. When the snow cover lasts late into the summer, *Vaccinium myrtillus* cannot grow and the reduced competition improves conditions for other species. In Alaska *Cladonia alpestris* suppresses even low shrubs, including *Empetrum nigrum* and *Vaccinium vitis-idaea,* but it

Figure 2-2. Invasion of a waste area by annual weeds: *Iva xanthifolia*, *Kochia scoparia*, *Bromus tectorum*, *Chenopodium* sp., *Polygonum aviculare*, and *Lactuca scariola*—a pioneer stage in secondary succession. June, Colorado.

does not grow as well as *C. rangiferina* in the shade of the taller shrub, *Betula glandulosa* (Figure 2-1).

The formation of weed groupings in early stages of succession in cultivated or abandoned fields is often closely related to environmental conditions.[75,160] Man has undoubtedly influenced the formation or modification of communities for a long time, and this continues now at an accelerated rate. The maqui vegetation of the Mediterranean region, the shiblyak of the Balkans, and the carbón scrub in Central America are apparently the result of man's interference.[4] The entire chaparral community in California seems to be in a state of flux, with variations of *Adenostoma fasciculatum,* hybrid manzanitas, hybrid oaks, and *Ceanothus* spp. in an ecologically disturbed habitat; but the extent to which it is man-made is not clear,[4] and further study by analytical methods, unbiased by preconceived dogmas, is required.

Seven basic ecological processes are involved in the formation of new groupings and in the modification of existing ones: migra-

Figure 2-3. Aggregation by growth of seedlings of *Pinus ponderosa* in an opening in the forest, showing a dense stand with excessive competition. Lassen National Forest, California. (U. S. Forest Service.)

Figure 2-4. An aggregation of the insectivorous pitcherplant (*Sarracenia flava*) in a marsh in Louisiana. (U.S.D.A. Soil Conservation Service.)

tion, germination, establishment (Figure 2-2), aggregation (Figures 2-3 and 2-4), competition and other coactions, reaction (Figure 2-5), and replacement. Migration can be by seed or by vegetative parts, the former often requiring more exacting conditions than the latter. Establishment or ecesis is considered accomplished when the plants are reproducing themselves, but many seedlings never succeed. Seedlings and vegetative offshoots tend to aggregate about the parents, and this leads to competition for light or other requirements, but some plants need the shade of others or the protection of shrubs from grazing in order to reach maturity. Usually the plants with the greatest competitive capacity have the best chance for survival. Reactions such as shading often make the environment less suitable for the present occupants of an area but more favorable for other species which may invade and become established. These processes are occurring continually in all plant groupings and in time lead to great changes during the course of ecological succession.

Figure 2-5. Sandreed (*Calamovilfa gigantea*) has formed a stand by means of the vigorous growth of rhizomes, now reacting on the habitat by stabilizing the sand movement. October, Woodward, Oklahoma. (U.S.D.A. Soil Conservation Service.)

A specific grouping of plants, including all the layers, is a **stand** (Figures 1-11 and 2-3). It may be defined as a particular aggregation of plants having a high degree of uniformity in composition and structure and occupying an area of essentially uniform environment. The terms **community, concrete community, individual community,** and **phytocenose** also refer to a specific grouping of plants, but "community" may also be used for any aggregation of plants. Within a more or less limited geographical area similar groupings of species occur in similar habitats, whereas different groupings are found under various combinations of environmental factors. Groupings are not identical, nor genetically related, even within a limited area, but some do resemble one another sufficiently, and differ from other groupings sufficiently, so they can be classified together as one **community type, abstract community,** or **association.** A community type or abstract community may be defined as a group of stands that are similar in species composition and structure and occupy similar habitats. An association, as defined by the Third International Botanical Congress in Brussels, is ". . . the fundamental unit of phytosociology, being a plant community of certain floristic composition, of uniform habitat conditions and of uniform physiognomy." [209] The association in the Clements sense is a subdivision of the formation, occupying a large area, and recognized or delimited by its floristics, physiognomy, and organic relation to other units in the formation.[41] Obviously, there is no correspondence between the two definitions.

The grouping of similar stands into one community type does not require that the composition, abundance, and structure of the stands be identical, nor that the habitats be identical; but it does require a certain degree of resemblance, more than with members of other community types (Figures 1-1 and 1-4). The similarity in habitats lies not necessarily in the homology of the soils, but in the similarity of conditions for plant growth, for a well-developed humus carbonate soil may support the same kind of vegetation as an iron podsol soil; the soils are analogous, not identical.[26] An example of similar stands in similar habitats is the intimate relationship that exists between vegetation and topography in Island Beach State Park, New Jersey. This relationship is especially constant in herbaceous stands which occupy facets characterized by limiting environmental conditions, such as dunegrass communities on primary foredunes, the true salt marsh occurring in intertidal peat flats, and nearly all the reedgrass communities on low sandy ridges parallel to the shoreline.[144] Neither does the concept of community type, or abstract community, require that all habitats resembling one another should be occupied by similar groupings, for such habitats may be so widely separated—grasslands in the Ukraine and in North America for example—that the constituent species of each have been prevented by natural barriers from migrating from one to the other. Vegetation in similar habitats may also differ because the stands are in various stages of succession or the sources of the disseminules may be located at various distances.

While the stands in a community type are not precisely alike, the inclusion of similar groupings under one category is most useful in the interpretation of relations between vegetation and environment, and is as logical as many other kinds of classification. The resemblance between stands is neither superficial nor accidental, as stated by Gleason,[90] but is often profound, as shown by the high degree of relationship between vegetation and environment as compared to other kinds of stands in the same geographic area. It seems impossible that each community is the product of its own independent causative factors,[90] for many interrelations between species in different stands do exist such as pollination, seed dispersal, feeding of animals, and the spreading of parasites. Because of these interrelationships a plant community cannot be a wholly individualistic entity—barriers completely isolating communities or ecosystems simply do not exist here.[70]

Since habitats differ; since species differ in their requirements, ecological amplitudes, and relations with other species; and because some habitats and stands are similar, it is to be expected that groupings of different degrees of resemblance can be made. Similarity in habitat is often indicated by the physiognomy, life-form, and structure of the vegetation, although the species composition may vary, as in various grasslands; e.g., the Great Plains biome belongs to the same grassland biome type as the South African, Central Asian, Brazilian, and other grassland biomes.[2]

It is possible that species of different life-forms, formerly isolated by geographic barriers, may succeed in new, closely similar habitats as shown by the ability of *Eucalyptus* spp., which form woodland in Australia, to persist in grassland in California.[10] It appears questionable, however, that *Eucalyptus* spp., planted in California, are steadily converting grassland into forest. It appears that usually the species best adapted in the long run to the complex physical conditions and to the species of plants and animals with which they are associated are those that have developed close interrelationships during the long period of evolution within a specific geographic area or ecosystem. Even though climates may be similar in geographically separated areas, other factors affecting vegetation and soils are likely to be dissimilar. When introduced species of different life-form grow successfully in a community, such as crested wheatgrass in native grassland in the northern Great Plains and possibly *Eucalyptus* in California, or when native species such as mesquite and cacti invade grasslands in the southwestern United States (Figure 1-12) or shortgrasses invade mixed and tallgrass prairie in Nebraska (as happened during the 1930 decade) it appears that there have been changes in environmental conditions or in associated species such as those caused by excessive grazing, drought, or even absence of fire. Dissimilarities in habitats commonly result in differences in the life-form and structure of the vegetation, as illustrated by biomes in different biome-types, and apparently this is true also in bryophytic communities.[85]

The classification of concrete communities or stands into abstract communities or community types is valid and useful, particularly within a limited geographic area and often in a large area, as demonstrated by numerous workers. The gradual transition of one group into another, forming a **continuum**,[60] which may be repeated in different locations in a large area, does not invalidate the classification of stands into abstract communities or types, but instead, seems to require the recognition of additional abstract types, separated from one another by arbitrary criteria.[200,206] Comparison may be made to Mendelian populations which are recognized although they are not necessarily discrete units, and often no sharp demarcation can be made between them. Likewise, youth and old age are recognized but they cannot be sharply segregated.

In a region where topographic changes are frequent, as in many hilly and mountainous sections, the vegetation at first glance appears chaotic—the heterogeneity seems to be without "rhyme or reason." The problem of individualizing and circumscribing groupings in the complex mosaic of vegetation is an old one in phytosociology. However, close inspection soon reveals that certain species are grouped together, although the proportions may differ in different sites. The groups may be segregated by sharp vegetational boundaries (ecotones) that may coincide with abrupt changes in physical conditions in the soil such as texture, structure, moisture content, or chemical constituents.[62,148] Other sharply delimited stands may be the result of fire, cultivation, animal activity, wind, or salt spray. Even in bogs sharp segregation is common,[72] but mosaic transitions may also occur.[153]

Where changes in environmental conditions are gradual the vegetation alters continuously from one kind of community to another. But even under such conditions, discontinuities are often present because one species may be the chief dominant in one part of the gradient, but in another part, where the critical point of tolerance has been reached, another kind suddenly takes its place; however, there may be a narrow sector of the gradient where both dominants are in competition.[11] In many areas both abrupt and gradual changes between communities are present. In an extensive study of forest succession in Algonkuin Park, Canada, Martin[143] concluded that because of the great diversity in the forests it is unfruitful to debate whether forest succession is a continuum or a series of distinct communities. In some circumstances it is a continuum, in others a series of communities; or it may be a continuum in one period, a distinct community in another. In most cases elements of both are present in varying proportions.

The vegetation and topography of a large part of western North Dakota show considerable heterogeneity (Figure 2-6) and will be discussed in detail here so as to serve as an example of the grouping of species.[106] In order to unravel relationships between plant groupings and topographic and soil conditions in this region, many stands were analyzed and described. The characteristics of frequency, abundance, and herbage cover were chiefly used to measure the degree of success of the plants in the different habitats, and the species were then grouped into nine main community types. The habitats differed in topography, thickness of the surface layer of dark soil, depth at which calcium carbonate showed effervescence with HCl, alkalinity or acidity of the upper horizons, total concentration of soluble salts, amounts of sodium and carbonate, soil texture, and colloidal content. On the upland plateaus and gentle upland slopes with a fairly deep, dark, residual sandy-loam soil (Chestnut group) the chief dominants and constants were *Bouteloua gracilis, Stipa comata, Carex filifolia, C. stenophylla, Agropyron smithii,* and *Koeleria cristata.* Stands of these and associated species occurring in different areas were sufficiently

Figure 2-6. Similar communities occur in similar habitats such as plateau tops, long slopes, valleys, and eroding banks. A stand of blue gramagrass-needle-and-thread-sedge community-type appears in the foreground. May, 1959, western North Dakota. (U.S.D.A. Soil Conservation Service.)

similar to be considered as one kind of community—the blue gramagrass-needlegrass-sedge community type—which occupied more of the region than any of the other types. Other groupings occurred on valley-fill deposits on long, gradual slopes of clay-loam soil with a shallow layer of dark soil; on steep slopes of clay-loam to loam with a shallow layer of dark soil; and on sandy soil. Many species possessed wide ecological amplitude, as indicated by their occurrence in different habitats, such as *Bouteloua gracilis, Agropyron smithii, Stipa comata, Koeleria cristata, Chenopodium leptophyllum, Artemisia frigida,* and *Gaura coccinea.* The first three were much more successful ecologically than the others, largely, it appears, because of their superior competitive capacity. On the other hand, a few species had a narrow range of ecological amplitude, or had little capacity to utilize the resources of any of the habitats of this region. Two of these, *Stipa spartea* and *Sporobolus heterolepis,* are better adapted to conditions farther east, i.e., those which the prairies provide as an environment more nearly within the range of their optimum ecological amplitudes. The big bluestem, or turkey-foot, *Andropogon gerardi,* grew in only one kind of habitat, which was restricted to the lower parts of steep slopes where the loam to sandy-loam soil was deep and moist; and here it was successful with *A. scoparius* and *Sporobolus heterolepis* as characteristic associates. *Puccinellia airoides,* because of its tolerance of poorly drained soil with a high content of soluble salts, utilized resources of low stream terraces where the conditions were outside the amplitude range of most of the species occurring in this region. *Distichlis stricta* was a common associate but, probably because of possessing greater competitive capacity, it grew also in association with *Agropyron smithii* and other species on better-drained terraces.

The number of species per community type in this region varied from about 20 to 29 in the less favorable habitats to 41 to 86 in the more favorable ones. Apparently many species were excluded from some habitats because of one or more limiting factors, and possibly because of insufficient competitive capacity when growing in environments near the limits of their ecological amplitude. Although grasses were usually dominant, 66 to 80 per cent of the total number of species in each community were usually forbs. The great variety of species in some stands, 86 in the *Andropogon gerardi* prairie type, was possible because the resources of the habitat were ample and because differences in life-form and season of maximum needs made association of diverse species possible. When the number of species was very low, as 12 per stand—averaging only 3.7 per square meter—it seems that more kinds could not grow because their requirements could not be provided by the habitat. These results support a probable rule that diversity of species and productivity are related to favorableness of environmental conditions, and the greater the number and diversity of species the greater will be the number and kinds of interrelations (reactions and coactions).

In alpine communities in the Arctic and Subarctic the same species often occur in many different communities, but the proportions of the various species change from one community to another. In one type of community one species is dominant, in a second type another is dominant, but the first species may also be present. The vegetation is not at all a chaotic assemblage. Similarly in grasslands in the Great Plains, blue gramagrass (*Bouteloua gracilis*) and western wheatgrass (*Agropyron smithii*) may both be present in two community types, but the former is dominant in one, the latter in the other because of soil differences, which may, however, cause only a slight change in the habitat as a whole. Even with a low number of species per stand many kinds of communities can be formed. For example, on the Cornish serpentine, only ten species were found to play an important part in determining the physiognomy and structure of the heaths as a whole, although 1023 combinations of them are possible. However, only four heaths are of cardinal ecological significance in this region, namely, *Festuca ovina-Calluna vulgaris* (rock heath), *Erica vagans-Ulex europaeus* (mixed heath), *Erica vagans-Schoenus nigricans* (tall heath), and *Agrostis setacea* (short heath).[51]

Six community types were recognized in the aspen groveland mosaic in Glacier County, Montana, on the basis of frequency, vitality, constancy, presence of species, and the age and height of the trees.[138] The endless number of variations of stands in the conifer-dominated forests of northern Idaho and adjacent Washington have been classified into 13 climax associations in four vegetation zones, each characterized by a particular combination of vascular plant unions ("union" being defined as "a group of plants exhibiting ecologic similarity throughout a particular vegetation matrix"). The vegetation consists of broad expanses with a low degree of variation, separated by narrow strips—but not as a continuum with pronounced gradients extending in all directions, nor as sharply defined discontinuities in the distribution of species.[66] In grasslands in western Canada, dominance, distribution of subdominants, and basal cover were mostly used in determining groupings.[57]

Important factors in causing the differential groupings of species into two major groups in an area in the lower foothills in northern Colorado appear to be deposition *versus* erosion, and differences in the gravel content in the 0- to 6-in. soil horizon.[103] The grouping on sites which showed evidence of deposition, with the gravel content averaging 2.2 per cent, consisted of the dominants *Agropyron smithii, Bouteloua gracilis,* and *Bromus tectorum* and a limited number of associates, averaging 11.2 species per stand. The groupings in the other major group were the dominants (a) *Stipa comata, Bouteloua gracilis,* and *B. curtipendula* with 28.7 species per stand; (b) *Andropogon scoparius* with 35 species per stand; and (c) *B. gracilis* and *Artemisia dracunculus* ssp. *glauca* with 21.6 species per stand. The gravel content averaged 33.0, 21.2, and 15.6 per cent, respectively, in this group, with evidence of slight to moderate erosion. The grouping of species in the *Agropyron-Bouteloua-Bromus* community appears to be related more to soil characteristics of the habitat than to interrelations of species, and the paucity of constants and the low number of species appear to be caused partly by the compactness of the soil, which hinders penetration of water. Many species of the other three communities do not occur in this one because adequate relations with the particular environmental conditions cannot apparently be established, but these three dominants are well adapted to utilize the resources present in this habitat, although they are more limited here than in the other three. However, in some years, when the soil moisture is low in the spring although ample later in the season, *Bromus tectorum* cannot germinate and grow well, with resulting reduction in abundance and height; but *Agropyron smithii* and *Bouteloua gracilis* are able to use the moisture that comes in later rains and therefore grow much better in the absence of severe competition with *Bromus tectorum*. It has been found that the germination of *B. tectorum* seeds is retarded by certain temperature conditions,[112] which may be a limiting factor in certain years for this bromegrass in this community.

GENERAL REFERENCES

Allee, W. C., *et al.*, "Principles of Animal Ecology," W. B. Saunders Co., Philadelphia, Pa., 1949.

Anderson, E., "Introgressive Hybridization," John Wiley & Sons, Inc., New York, N.Y., 1949.

Conard, H. S., "The Background of Plant Ecology" (trans. from the German of Kerner, A., 1863, "The Plant Life in the Danube Basin"), Iowa State Col. Press, Ames, Iowa, 1951.

Dahl, E., "Rondane, Mountain Vegetation in South Norway and Its Relation to the Environment," Aschehoug & Co., Oslo, 1956.

Tansley, A. G., "The British Islands and their Vegetation," 2 Vols., Cambridge Univ. Press, Cambridge, 1949.

PART TWO

The Community

ANALYTIC CHARACTERISTICS
OF THE COMMUNITY

The characteristics of a community may be conveniently classified into two main groups, analytic and synthetic. The analytic group, to be discussed in this chapter, includes qualitative characteristics, which are usually described because of the greater difficulty in measuring them, and quantitative ones, which can be readily measured. These characteristics are as follows:

(1) Qualitative
   (a) Kinds of species in the community (floristic composition)
   (b) Stratification (of organisms, or their parts, above or below ground)
   (c) Periodicity (phenology, aspection)
   (d) Vitality (vigor)
   (e) Life-form (vegetation-, habitat-, and growth-form)
   (f) Sociability (gregariousness)
   (g) Association of species (interspecific association)

(2) Quantitative

  (a) Population density (number of individuals, abund-
      ance)
  (b) Cover (area occupied)
  (c) Height of plants
  (d) Weight of plants
  (e) Volume occupied by plants
  (f) Frequency

QUALITATIVE CHARACTERISTICS

Kinds of Species Occurring in the Community (Floristic Composition)

A complete list of species is the most essential characteristic of
a stand, and the making of such a list is the first step in its study.
In practice it is impossible to name all the organisms in a bio-
cenose, so botanists usually name only the vascular plants, but it
is essential to include the cryptophytes, especially lichens and
mosses, in many communities, particularly in arctic and alpine regions. In order to secure a complete list, inspection and collecting
throughout the growing season are required so that all species
appearing in different seasons will be included. The plants need
to be correctly named, which often requires the aid of a compe-
tent, systematic botanist, and herbarium specimens prepared for
future reference and as vouchers. In areas where little ecological
work has been done, or where time does not permit detailed
study, lists accompanied by accurate descriptions of the whole
area may be of more value than detailed records in only one or a
few localities.

Floristic lists are valuable for characterization because each
species has its own range of ecological amplitude (Figure 3-1).
Each one has its particular relationships to the environment and
to other species, so the total number of species, as well as the
average number per sample area in each stand, tell much about
the conditions of the habitat. For example, 36 species were present in a certain number of nongrazed sample areas in virgin tallgrass prairie in central Oklahoma, while 64 species were found
in the same number of sample areas in the grazed part, indicat-

Figure 3-1. The kinds of species and life-forms are numerous and varied in some desert communities, growing in the summer or the winter rainy periods in the southwestern United States. The saguaro (*Carnegiea gigantea*) has fair frequency. Superstition Mountains in background. Arizona. (U.S.D.A. Soil Conservation Service.)

ing that a decrease in the abundance of dominant prairie plants and a lessening of their competitive capacity had permitted many invaders to become established. In 60 sq m of a western wheatgrass range under deferred and rotation grazing in Colorado, 75 species were present, while in the adjoining continuously grazed pasture 76 were found in the same number of quadrats. The difference in grazing intensity evidently was not as great between the two pastures in Colorado as between the grazed and nongrazed prairie areas in Oklahoma. Although all the species in a stand are significant, a single species is often used in naming a vegetation type because of its abundance or dominance—such as creosote bush (*Larrea divaricata*) in Arizona deserts. However, the use of additional species, at least the chief dominants of the various layers, is preferable.

Often in descriptions of vegetation only the more abundant, dominant, or "most important" species are listed, and only the number instead of the names of "unimportant" species is given, even though the plants in the latter group may make up a considerable proportion of the vegetation. It is essential scientifically and more useful practically, to include all species, because some which appear insignificant at the time of the investigation may indicate conditions that existed at an earlier time but are not present now; or they may indicate, as "prediction species," a future trend. Complete lists furnish material for, and are frequently used by, later investigators in ways not considered by the original worker. All species play some part in a stand, and no investigator has the right to presume unimportance in Nature; for example, the cutleaf violet (*Viola pedatifida*) is considered one of the best indicators of tallgrass prairie conditions in Iowa, although it is inconspicuous and has little or no forage value compared to the tall bunch grasses.[7]

Other small plants often appearing insignificant, such as mosses and lichens in the Arctic and Subarctic (see Figure 2-1), have narrow but different ranges of amplitude, so they are particularly valuable as indicators of soil and microclimatic conditions, of overgrazing by reindeer or caribou, or of successional status. Herbaceous forest plants, although often inconspicuous, are more delicate indicators of soil conditions than trees, and have been used in the delimitation of communities.[33] In rich mesophytic forests in the eastern United States, mull humus supports a luxuriant herbaceous flora including *Viola canadensis, V. palmata, Phacelia bipinnatifida, Disporum lanuginosum,* and several ferns; while mor humus, especially characteristic of coniferous forests, has a different, sparse flora including *Lycopodium* spp., *Cornus canadensis, Maianthemum canadense,* and *Trillium undulatum.*[22] Another example of the importance of the so-called "insignificant" species is seen in southern Arizona, where minor grasses of the mesa-range type, although each one makes up less than 1 per cent of

Figure 3-2. A conspicuous layer is formed by the flowering dogwood (*Cornus florida*) in the deciduous forest, occurring from Maine to northeastern Mexico; a pronounced spring aspect. May 10, 1957, near Chester, New Jersey. (U.S.D.A. Soil Conservation Service.)

the stand, are important economically because in the aggregate they form 10 per cent of the total grass cover on conservatively grazed ranges, and as the grassland improves they become more numerous.[35] These species (characteristic species of Braun-Blanquet) may also be important in delimiting and describing plant communities.[11,24,25] These various examples illustrate the importance of finding and recording all species in a stand, for the absence of some and the presence of others may indicate present conditions and future trends.

A decline in the number of species from one area to another may indicate increasingly adverse conditions. For example, the number of species in xeric grasslands in Colorado changes greatly with increasing elevation; 160 species were found in the mountain front at 5300 ft, 139 in the foothills at 7500 ft, 130 in the upper foothills at 8400 ft, and only 50 in the subalpine zone at

11,500 ft.[168] In the *Andropogon scoparius* grassland on the Hemp-stead Plains, Long Island, 71 species were recorded,[32] while in western North Dakota, where a similar community type is usually restricted to north-facing slopes, the average number per stand was only 50.[106] Similarly, many alpine communities in central Europe have more species than those in Scandinavia. The mere listing of species without data on relative abundance, however, may be misleading, for some species often occur in different pro-portions in various communities, particularly in the Arctic and Subarctic. Even though the number of species per stand is as low as 12 to 20, the number of kinds of communities that can develop is enormous.

Stratification

Stratification, or layering, is the occurrence of organisms, or their parts, at different levels in a stand. Stratification is readily seen above ground, but is present also in the unseen root systems and rhizomes. Stratification usually occurs because life-forms such as trees, shrubs, herbs, and mosses differ in their require-ments and amplitudes, and therefore grow at various levels which differ in light intensity, temperature, moisture conditions, organic content of the soil, and other factors (Figures 2-1 and 3-2).

The number of strata above ground vary according to the kind of community. In early stages of succession usually only one stratum is present, comprising such plants as lichens, mosses, or annual herbs; but as succession proceeds additional strata appear, so that in a mature grassland there may be three strata, the two highest comprising grasses and forbs, and the lowest short herbs, mosses, lichens, and occasionally algae. Five to seven strata may be found in forests: two or three of trees, one or two of shrubs, an herb or field layer, and a ground or moss-lichen layer (Figures 1-2 and 1-16). Occasional trees that project above the general canopy are called **emergent** or **supercanopy** trees. The chief layer in savannas is the field layer of herbs or sometimes low shrubs; the scattered trees or tall shrubs hardly form a layer.

Stratification is well developed in tropical rain forests. For ex-ample, in Nigeria the top tree layer at 120 to 150 ft consists of relatively few species with wide-spreading, umbrella-shaped crowns as much as 80 ft in diameter that do not touch one another. The middle layer at 50 to 120 ft contains many species with small, rounded crowns up to 33 ft in diameter that occasionally come into contact. The lowest stratum, as high as 50 feet, is limited in the number of trees that are restricted to this level, but contains many young individuals belonging to species characteristic of the two upper layers. The crowns are often small and conical with larger leaves than the taller trees, and they form a closed canopy bound together by climbing plants. The shrub layer, containing mostly young trees and a few shrubs, is poorly defined. The herb layer, not over 3 ft high, is even more poorly deliniated and in places is missing. The ground layer is missing entirely.[170]

In the Mixed Mesophytic Forest region of the Cumberland Mountains, and in the southern Allegheny Mountains and adjacent territory, the top layer of trees varies in composition in different areas. The dominants in this region total about 25 species and include the beech (*Fagus grandifolia*), tulip tree (*Liriodendron tulipifera*), basswood (*Tilia heterophylla, T. floridana, T. neglecta*), sugar maple (*Acer saccharum*), sweet buckeye (*Aesculus octandra*), and white oak (*Quercus alba*). In the lower tree layer are found dogwood (*Cornus florida*), magnolia (*Magnolia tripetala, M. macrophylla*), redbud (*Cercis canadensis*), blue beech (*Carpinus caroliniana*), hornbeam (*Ostrya virginiana*), holly (*Ilex opaca*), striped maple (*Acer pennsylvanicum*), and others. Many species are found in the shrub layer, such as *Lindera benzoin, Hamamelis virginiana, Asimina triloba, Hydrangea arborescens*, and *Cornus alternifolia*. The field layer is very rich in herbs which are favored by the mull humus developed from leaf litter of the trees, and the spring aspect is noted for conspicuous flowering plants such as *Trillium grandiflorum, T. erectum, Viola* spp., *Sanguinaria canadensis*, and *Erythronium americanum*. In late summer and autumn, the fall asters (*Aster cordifolius, A. divaricatus*) and goldenrods (*Solidago caesia, S. lalifolia*) come into bloom.[22]

Stratification in a jack pine community in Quebec, a stage following a forest fire, consists of four layers. The upper layer of trees, 10 to 35 ft high and about 25 ft apart, comprises chiefly *Pinus banksiana*, and a few *Betula papyrifera* var. *cordifolia* and *Picea mariana*. The second stratum has the same kinds of trees, 3 to 10 ft high and 10 to 25 ft apart; and the third consists mostly of *Comptonia peregrina* and scattered *Pteridium aquilinum* ssp. *latiuscula, Vaccinium canadense,* and *Solidago puberula,* 1 to 3 ft high and less than 2 ft apart. The fourth layer, 6 to 12 in. high, is made up chiefly of clumps of *Gaultheria procumbens* and *Lycopodium tristachyum,* about 1 ft in diameter and 6 ft apart.[63]

In the primeval spruce forest in the Medicine Bow Mountains of Wyoming, the canopy layer comprises the Engelmann spruce (*Picea engelmanni*) and subalpine fir (*Abies lasiocarpa*), the latter being more numerous. The second tree layer is represented only by scattered spruce and fir trees which do not penetrate the canopy. The shrub layer, 2 to 3 ft high, is poorly developed, and the field layer has about 20 species of herbs and one low shrub, *Vaccinium scoparium,* less than 2 ft high. This shrub is especially significant because tree seedlings are seldom found in its dense clumps. Mosses and lichens make up the ground layer.[157]

Grassland in good condition often shows well developed stratification, as exemplified by the gramagrass-needlegrass-sedge grassland in western North Dakota, in which the uppermost layer consists of *Stipa comata* and a few scattered forbs. The second layer is a mixture that includes *Agropyron smithii, Carex stenophylla, Koeleria cristata,* and *Calamagrostis montanensis.* The lowest layer is represented by the mat-forming grasses, *Bouteloua gracilis* and *Carex filifolia,* and by low forbs such as *Plantago purshii* and *Hedeoma hispida.* Another layer of clubmosses and lichens may occur in places.[106]

The composition of the vegetation in each layer may vary from place to place so that distinct groups of plants similar in life-form, called **synusiae,** or unions[67] are recognizable. Examples of synusiae are stands of *Polytrichum* moss in the ground layer of an open oak forest and a stand of *Vaccinium* sp. in the low shrub layer of a pine woods. Different synusiae may appear in the same layer at various seasons of the year, for example, mosses and lichens may form winter synusiae and *Antennaria* sp. summer synusiae in *Andro-*

pogon stands in eastern Maryland. They should always be considered as part of the stand as a whole, instead of as independent units, because numerous interactions take place between many organisms in the different layers. All the synusiae and layers are closely integrated with the entire stand.

Plants in the lower strata may increase in size and number when those in the upper stratum are removed by grazing or mowing. For example, in ungrazed prairie in Missouri the short *Antennaria neglecta* and *Viola sagittata* made up 1 to 4, and 0.4, per cent of the stand, respectively, while in the grazed and mowed prairie they made up 9.3 and 3.1 per cent respectively. Other components of the lowest stratum, *Trifolium pratense, T. repens,* and *Oxalis stricta,* were also abundant in the latter.[71] Big sagebrush (*Artemisia tridentata*) suppresses all plants in the stand when its crowns cover about 40 per cent of the ground,[173] but when it has been destroyed by burning, uprooting, or spraying with an herbicide, the plants in the field layer usually flourish and provide much forage.

Layering of root systems may be caused by various factors, such as differences in moisture content of the soil and the concentration of salts at various depths. This is common in many parts of the western United States. For example, in the vicinity of Milford, Utah, three layers were evident: (1) the uppermost layer, to a depth of 30 to 45 cm, with a salt concentration of less than 1000 ppm (bridge method) in which the roots of *Bouteloua gracilis, Hilaria jamesii,* and *Sporobolus cryptandrus* were restricted; (2) an intermediate layer, at between 40 and 65 cm, where the salt content was over 1000 ppm and in which were found some of the larger roots of *Atriplex confertifolia, Chrysothamnus stenophyllus,* and *Eurotia lanata;* and (3) the lowest layer, at 80 to 90 cm, where the soil was more porous and contained less salt, and where roots of *Artemisia tridentata* and *Grayia spinosa* were found.[185]

Periodicity (Phenology, Aspection)

Periodicity refers to the regular seasonal occurrence of various processes such as photosynthesis, growth, pollination, flowering, and ripening of fruits and seeds; and the manifestations of

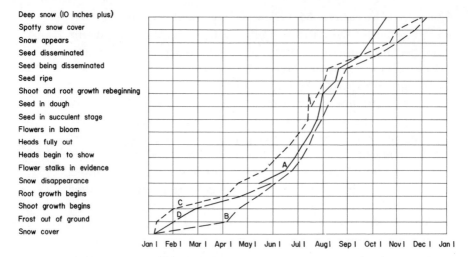

Deep snow (IO inches plus)
Spotty snow cover
Snow appears
Seed disseminated
Seed being disseminated
Seed ripe
Shoot and root growth rebeginning
Seed in dough
Seed in succulent stage
Flowers in bloom
Heads fully out
Heads begin to show
Flower stalks in evidence
Snow disappearance
Root growth begins
Shoot growth begins
Frost out of ground
Snow cover

Jan I Feb I Mar I Apr I May I Jun I Jul I Aug I Sep I Oct I Nov I Dec I Jan I

Chart 3. Phenological events in the annual growth of mountain bromegrass (*Bromus carinatus*) in Ephraim Canyon, Wasatch Mountains, Utah, during the four years: (A) 1932; (B) 1933; (C) 1934; (D) 1935. (After McCarty, E. C. (138A), "The Relation of Growth to the Varying Carbohydrate Content in Mountain Brome," Figure 3, *U. S. Dept. Agric. Tech. Bull.*, No. 598, 1–24 (1938).)

these processes, such as formation of leaves, elongation of shoots, appearance of flowers, and dissemination of seeds (see Chart 3). Periodicity results from inherent genetic characteristics of each species under the influence of a particular combination of environmental conditions. **Periodicity** means particularly the recurrence at certain times of these processes and their manifestations, while **phenology** refers more to the appearance of the manifestations at certain seasons of the year (Figure 3-2), rather than to their cyclic nature. **Aspection** is the appearance or aspect of the community as a whole at different seasons. Periodicity is a strongly fixed character in plants, for even in portions of the Tropics where great uniformity in climate prevails, it is apparent in the fall of leaves at certain intervals and also in periods of intensive growth followed by dormancy.

Periodicity is not readily altered even though climatic conditions change. Correspondence in climatic and life-cycle periodicities indicates the location of the native home of a plant, whereas if such correspondence is lacking, either the climate has changed or the plant has very likely been transferred from its original home. For example, in Czechoslovakia the autumn crocus, *Colchicum autumnale,* a native of the Mediterranean Region, flowers in the autumn and ripens fruit in the spring, contrary to the behavior of its associates which bloom and fruit in the same year. The great diversity in periodicity among species in the present flora of Europe can be explained by the great climatic changes that have occurred there, accompanied by migrations of species. The oaks, *Quercus robur* and *Q. sessiliflora,* and the beech, *Fagus sylvatica,* apparently were adapted in the past to a warmer climate and have not yet, even after thousands of years, become adapted to the climatic rhythm of their present environment. This lack of complete adaptation is revealed in the abscission layer remaining alive and green during the entire winter, and in the falling of their leaves, which coincides with the development of new leaf-buds, similar to the habit of the evergreen broad-leaved species. Plants which do not pass through a full cycle of development, or a normal development, indicate that they originated in some other kind of community than the one of which they now form a part, as exemplified by the failure to flower of *Caltha palustris* in a dry meadow, or the failure of *Vaccinium uliginosum* to flower and fruit in Novaya Zemlya.

Most communities have a definite aspect at different seasons of the year. The chief aspects are the **prevernal,** or early spring; the **vernal,** or spring; the **aestival,** or summer; the **serotinal,** or autumn; and the **hiemal** or **hibernal,** winter. It is interesting to keep records of phenological events such as the dates of appearance of certain kinds of seedlings in various years, the inception of growth of perennials, the opening of leaf and flower buds on certain trees, the full expansion of the leaves, and the appearance of first flowers, first ripe fruits, last flowers, and the completion of the dissemination of the fruits or seeds. Each species and each stage has its own specific rate of development and growth. These physiological phenomena have practical value in integrating many environmental factors, and can then be used to predict the time of harvest, when a range is ready for grazing, and other practices.

Environmental factors have great influence on phenological behavior. For example, in the southern Arizona desert (Figures 1-12 and 3-1) plants begin to grow as soon as the temperature is high enough in late winter or spring, and if there is enough moisture the desert blooms with the yellow flowers of Mexican poppy (*Eschscholtzia neomexicana*), pink penstemon (*Penstemon parryi*), blue lupines (*Lupinus* spp.), yellow bladder-pod (*Lesquerella gordoni*), asters (*Aster* spp.), mariposa lily (*Calochortus aureus*), mustards, and many others. Outstanding forage plants at this season are Indian wheat (*Plantago argyrea*) and alfilaria (*Erodium cicutarium*), the latter a native of the Mediterranean Region. Growth ceases for these plants, many of which have shallow roots, when the April-June drought period sets in. The July rains bring on the growth of summer annuals and many perennials, including the annuals, six-weeks grama (*Bouteloua barbata*) and needle grama (*B. aristidoides*), which take the place of Indian wheat and alfilaria as forage plants.[179]

Phenologic events may vary considerably in time of occurrence from year to year. Over a period of 10 years in southern Idaho the date of inception of growth varied from March 20 to April 24, growth of herbage to a height of 6 in. fluctuated between April 26 and June 1, and formation of seeds, from May 12 to July 10.[59] In the Wasatch Plateau in Utah inception of growth varied as much as 45 days in various years, and a height growth of 6 to 8 in. of the chief grasses—the height considered suitable for the initiation of the grazing season—varied as much as 47 days.[56] Altitude also influences phenologic behavior, as seen again in the Wasatch Mountains, where the rate of development of plant growth was delayed 10 to 14 days for each increase of 1000 ft.[56]

Phenologic behavior influences competition and association of species. The occurrence of vegetative growth, flowering, and fruiting at different seasons, or only slight overlapping of these activities, often reduces the intensity of competition and favors association. For example, *Agropyron* spp., *Poa* spp., and *Bromus tectorum* start growth and mature earlier than *Bouteloua gracilis*, with resulting reduction in competition, because the last has a higher threshold for inception of growth and a greater heat re-

Figure 3-3. A late summer aspect of an almost pure stand of tobosa grass (*Hilaria mutica*) in Graham County, Arizona, showing good response to summer rains. Density, height, herbage cover, and weight indicate excellent cover of the grass. Savanna type with scattered mesquite trees in the background; overgrazing, however, alters it to woodland. (U. S. Forest Service.)

quirement. A long growing season with ample soil moisture throughout is conducive to the formation of a community rich in species because great opportunity is provided for their growth at different times. The prairie, rich in habitat resources, therefore, can support a large number of species, in contrast to the habitats of shortgrass vegetation, which are deficient, especially in soil moisture.

Phenological events are usually well coordinated with environmental conditions in a community in the final stage of succession (Figure 3-3). Such a community uses so fully the resources of the habitat that it may be considered closed or saturated, so that other species cannot invade; in fact, many of the species within it cannot survive unless their main periods of growth, blooming, and other activities, do not coincide. Even then, competition within a community may become so severe that a species may survive only in an area outside of its optimum range, where competition is reduced because it grows in a different season from most of the plants in that community.[212]

It may be concluded that the various expressions of periodicity and phenology of plants are means of adaptation to seasonal changes in the physical environment. Usually, in order to live in a given location, the plant must make full use of the favorable environmental periods and endure or tolerate, by one means or another, the unfavorable periods.

Vitality (Vigor)

Vitality relates to the condition of a plant and its capacity to complete the life cycle, while **vigor** refers more specifically to the state of health or development within a certain stage; a seedling or mature plant may be vigorous, or it may be feeble and poorly developed (Figures 1-2, 1-19, 1-26). In order to appraise the degree of vigor one needs to know the appearance of normal plants, preferably under optimum conditions, in the various stages of growth. The vigor of species that are represented by only a few individuals in a stand often merits special attention because they may indicate the end of a previous stage of succession, the beginning of a new stage, a change in conditions such as an increase or decrease in soil moisture, attack by parasites, or some kind of harmful grazing practice. One of the first signs in the improvement of a depleted grassland in the annual weed stage is the appearance of scattered, newly established, vigorous perennial forbs and grasses.

A number of criteria may be used in determining the vigor of plants such as the rate and total amount of growth, especially in height; rapidity of growth renewal in the spring or following mowing or grazing; quantity or area of foliage; color and turgidity of leaves and stems; degree of damage by disease or insects; time of appearance and number and height of flower stalks; rate of growth and extent of the root system; appearance and development of new stems and leaves; and the extent of dead portions, especially in bunch- or mat-formers.

The following classification of vitality has been widely used: [24,25]

Class 1: Well-developed plants which regularly complete their life cycles

Class 2: Vigorous plants which usually do not complete their life cycles or are poorly developed, and sparsely distributed plants that do spread vegetatively

Class 3: Feeble plants that never complete their life cycles but do spread vegetatively

Class 4: Plants occasionally appearing from seed but which do not increase in number, such as ephemeral plants

As an example of the use of this classification, the species in an *Andropogon scoparius* stand on Long Island were classified as follows: 20 in class 1, 3 in class 2, 1 in class 3, and 2 in class 4, with two remaining unclassified.[46] The large number of species in class 1 indicates that the resources of this site were very good, permitting the functioning of many interactions without serious handicap from competition. When a species is not growing within its range of ecological amplitude, or when the competition with other plants is too severe, one of the first indications is the failure to bloom and fruit.

The vitality and vigor, as well as phenologic behavior, may be used to differentiate between ecotypes. For example, five climatic ecotypes of *Deschampsia caespitosa* ssp. *genuina,* all morphologically similar in their natural environments, were grown experimentally in one environment where they differed in height of the tallest stems, number of flower stalks, diameter of the clumps, time of flowering and fruiting, and susceptibility to frost and disease.[133] An ecotype growing outside of its natural environment will usually not be so vigorous as when growing within it. During the course of evolution the habitat requirements of ecotypes apparently became increasingly exacting, so ecotypes, rather than species, are the best indicators of ecological conditions. Species of wide distribution such as *Andropogon scoparius* and *Bouteloua curtipendula,* which grow in a variety of habitats, are often represented by a number of ecotypes with special adaptations enabling them to grow under different conditions of length of day, temperature, and soil moisture; but *Stipa spartea* and *Elymus canadensis* apparently respond to conditions in widely separated areas not because of genetic differences among the plants of each, but because of the wide range of phenotypic expression of the same genotype.[140,141]

Life-form (Vegetation-form, Habitat-form, Growth-form)

By life-form, in a broad sense, is meant the characteristic vegetative appearance such as the size, shape, branching, and at times the histological features of the plant body and its longevity. In a restricted sense it refers to the forms based on the location of the overwintering parts.[169] The life-form of a species is caused primarily by its genetic constitution, secondarily by the environmental conditions. Pronounced changes in the latter may cause great alterations in life-form. For example, the longevity of many perennial grasses may be reduced, as when rescuegrass (*Bromus catharticus*), a 4- to 5-year perennial in South America, was introduced into the southern United States. Here it became a winter annual, and when introduced into northern latitudes, an annual.[201]

The life-form influences the economic value of plants in various ways. For example, strains of grasses having a genetically determined wide leaf to stem ratio and low height, are preferred for pastures because of their greater nutritional value. The Fairway strain of crested wheatgrass (*Agropyron cristatum*), much used in reseeding range land, is smaller, more decumbent, and finer-leaved than the Standard strain. Prostrate forms of legumes are often preferred in pastures because some of the flowers usually escape grazing and produce seeds. These examples illustrate that the selection of suitable life-forms is an important objective in plant breeding.

All the species in a simple plant community may belong to the same life-form, but most communities have several to many (see Figures 2-5 and 3-1). Grassland stands in the Great Plains include various kinds of life-forms such as perennial rhizomatous mat-formers (*Bouteloua gracilis*), erect rhizomatous perennials (*Agropyron smithii*), perennial bunchgrasses (*Stipa comata*), succulent perennials (*Opuntia* spp.), small annuals (*Festuca octoflora*), and various short and tall forbs. The kinds of life-forms, the number of individuals of each kind, and their spacing give structure to the community.

The type of life-form has considerable influence on the association of species. In pastures in England, grasses are less favorable means of infection of sheep by worms than red and white clovers because the lower blades of the grasses present more obstacles to the worm when it is climbing up from the ground than the straight leafstalks of the clovers. A stand of late-maturing grasses often provides good opportunity for the growth of early-maturing forbs. Head smut (*Ustilago marginatus*) has been found to be more prevalent on a strain of *Bromus marginatus* characterized by early maturity and moderate leafiness, and less prevalent on a late-maturing, very leafy strain.

The general appearance of a community is caused more by the life-form of the most abundant or dominant species than by any other characteristic of the vegetation (Figure 1-16), so it is not surprising that it has been used very widely for description. Of the many classifications that have been proposed, Raunkiaer's simple system[169] is the most widely known and used. It is based upon the overwintering parts or the location of organs that survive summer drought or other unfavorable conditions. This classification, as modified somewhat by Braun-Blanquet,[25] comprises ten main classes, as follows:

(1) Phytoplankton: Microscopic plants suspended in air, water, or on snow
(2) Phytoedaphon: Microscopic soil flora
(3) Endophytes: Plants living wholly or partly within other plants, as algae in lichens, or parasites
(4) Therophytes: Annuals, including algae, fungi, liverworts, mosses, and many ferns and seed plants (Figure 1-7)
(5) Hydrophytes: All water plants, except plankton, with perennating parts submerged in water during unfavorable periods
(6) Geophytes: Plants with perennating parts buried in the substratum, such as species with rhizomes or bulbs (Figure 2-5)

(7) Hemicryptophytes: Plants with perennial shoots and buds close to the surface, often covered with litter, such as bunchgrasses and many forbs (Figure 1-2)

(8) Chamaephytes: Plants with buds located from the ground surface to 25 cm above it, such as buffalograss and white clover (Figure 1-13)

(9) Phanerophytes: Shrubs, trees, and vines with buds located on upright shoots at least 25 cm above the surface (Figures 2-3 and 3-2)

(10) Epiphytes: Plants growing on other plants (Figure 1-25)

Most of these classes have been subdivided.

All the species in a region or in a community can be classified into these classes and the ratio expressed in numbers or percentages, forming a floristic **biological spectrum.** This classification is very useful in comparing communities. For example, grasslands are usually rich in hemicryptophytes, tropical deserts in therophytes, and arctic and alpine regions in chamaephytes and hemicryptophytes. In comparing communities, however, the number of species is less satisfactory as a basis for establishing a vegetational spectrum than frequency points, because the former is based on the mere presence of the species in a community, while the frequency-point spectrum is based on the sum of the frequencies in each of the life-form classes. Relative cover may also be used in determining the vegetational spectrum. The advantage of the frequency method was demonstrated in hardwood forests in Minnesota where *Carex pennsylvanica* occurred in 94 quadrats out of a total of 100 in 10 stands, and since it is a cryptophyte it contributed 94 points to this class; but *Clintonia borealis,* occurring in only 3 quadrats, contributed only 3 points to the total of 97 points in this class. In the species-presence list,

	Chamaephytes, %	Hemicryptophytes, %	Cryptophytes, %	Therophytes, %
Species list	4.3	68.8	26.9	0
Frequency points	3.6	60.4	36.0	0

however, each species contributed one point each in the total of two. Differences between the two methods for herbaceous phanerogams are shown in the table on page 94. The frequency-point spectrum in this region emphasizes the importance of the better-protected life-form classes as compared to the species-list spectrum. The influence of the drier, more continental climate in Minnesota, in comparison to the moister climate in the mixed mesophytic forests of the southern Appalachians, can also be shown.[28]

Habitat-forms bear the impress of the habitat, such as cacti in arid climates (Figure 3-1) or Elodea submerged in water. These forms are mainly ecological and are of special value as indicators of environmental conditions. They can also be used in the analysis and characterization of communities, but have not been used extensively. The most common classification contains three classes: **hydrophytes,** which include submerged, floating, and amphibious plants; **mesophytes,** which include sun and shade plants; and **xerophytes,** which may be divided into groups on the basis of ability to endure drought. Every species has its own range of ecological amplitude, so by knowing the kinds of species that make up a stand one can evaluate the environmental conditions to a considerable degree. For instance, a stand of *Distichlis stricta* usually indicates a higher salt content and a shallower water-table than a stand of this grass intermixed with *Agropyron smithii*, while a stand of the latter as the sole dominant indicates little or no salt.

The detailed classification of habitat-forms by Iverson[114] includes four main divisions: land, swamp, amphibious, and water plants. The land plants comprise the following five classes: (1) seasonal xerophytes, as *Sedum* spp., which have shallow root systems and considerable tolerance to endure long periods without absorbing water; (2) euxerophytes with well developed root systems but which wilt quickly when absorption of water ceases, subdivided into four subclasses; (3) hemixerophytes with poorer root systems which also wilt quickly, subdivided into four subclasses; (4) mesophytes with poor, quick-wilting root systems; and (5) hygrophytes, plants of wet areas such as the marsh marigold

(*Caltha palustris*). This classification has been used advantageously in analyzing many plant communities (see the table below).

	Euxerophytes, %	Hemixerophytes, %	Mesophytes, %	Hygrophytes, %
Deschampsia caespitosa wet meadow	0	33	48	19
Agrostis tenuis dry meadow	12	15	62	8

Growth-form (phenotypic-form) refers to the development of plants of the same species under different environmental conditions. In abandoned fields in the Great Plains, Russian thistle (*Salsola kali*) may be 2 ft high, while in adjacent grasslands the tallest plants are only an inch or two in height because of their inability to compete with the perennial grasses. The growth-form of a species may also vary greatly within a single stand because of differences in microhabitats. Under heavy grazing, perennial rhizome grasses become smaller, more prostrate, and form a short, dense turf; while bunch grasses become reduced in size, with fewer and finer stems and leaves per plant, and with the clumps sometimes broken into smaller, separated tufts. As a consequence, in some grasslands the growth-form has been considered a more reliable indicator of grazing use than cover.

Sociability (Gregariousness)

Sociability refers to the proximity of plants or shoots to one another. It is dependent upon the life-form and vigor of the plants, habitat conditions, and competitive and other relations between individuals. The Braun-Blanquet scale,[25] given below, for rating sociability of species, has been widely used in analyzing vegetation.

Class 1: Shoots growing singly

Class 2: Small groups of plants such as *Chenopodium* spp., or scattered tufts, such as *Aristida* spp. (Figure 2-2)

Class 3: Small, scattered patches or cushions, e.g., patches of gramagrass or buffalograss, or large clumps of prickly pear cactus (Figure 1-4)

Class 4: Large patches or broken mats (Figure 1-16)

Class 5: Very large mats or stands of nearly pure populations that almost completely cover a large area, such as a *Vaccinium* heath, an *Andropogon scoparius* grassland, or a cattail marsh (Figures 1-6 and 1-13)

Other scales that use the actual areas occupied by groups have also been proposed.[11]

The shoots or plants of some species are able to grow much closer together than those of others, notably those that propagate by rhizomes, runners, or roots, forming very dense stands in which the shoots are separated by short internodes, Kentucky bluegrass for example. Species with longer internodes, such as smooth bromegrass, form more open stands. Also important in the forming of dense stands is the ability of shoots to tolerate shading, root competition, or some other adverse factor such as high humidity, which may favor infection by disease-producing organisms. Species that spread only by seed may also show a high degree of sociability, especially in the early stages of succession, as in abandoned fields where certain annual weeds may become very dense. The ability of these plants to form dense groups is related to the number of seeds produced, the mobility of seeds or fruits, the rate of germination, and the ability of seedlings and growing plants to survive disease and intense competition. *Bromus tectorum*, an annual, has been highly successful in invading large areas of western grasslands, forming stands with sociability of class 5. *Salsola kali* and *Chenopodium album* may also rate in class 5 in early stages of succession on abandoned fields, but in later stages they are usually reduced to class 1. Even annuals with fruits or seeds lacking special structures for dispersal, such as *C. album* and sunflowers (*Helianthus* spp.) often form dense aggregations because the seeds fall close to the parent; but species with very effective devices for dispersal, such as *Tragopogon pratensis*, are more likely to rate in class 1, unless they migrate into particularly favorable habitats.

Vegetative propagation is conducive to aggregation and often gives invaders pronounced advantages in becoming established (Figure 1-19). The new shoots on the rhizomes or runners are sustained by the parent plant during the time that new roots and leaves are forming, and thus are able to carry on competition advantageously with plants already present in the area. For example, the rhizomes of *Agropyron smithii* were undoubtedly a great aid in the invasions of the Nebraska prairies during the great 1930–1940 drought, when nearly pure, large populations, rating class 5, were formed. Certain species such as *Bouteloua gracilis, Aristida longiseta, Artemisia frigida,* and *Astragalus missouriensis* have a higher class of sociability under continuous grazing than under deferred and rotation grazing, while the opposite is true for *Agropyron smithii, Schedonnardus paniculatus, Eurotia lanata,* and *Senecio perplexus.*[105] Under some conditions such as severe grazing, shallow-rooted plants may invade and become very dense, replacing the former deep-rooted ones.

Association of Species

Association of species, or interspecific association, is the growing together of two or more species in close proximity to one another as a rather regular occurrence; for example, Kentucky bluegrass and white clover in many pastures, *Stipa comata* and *Bouteloua gracilis* in some grasslands in the Great Plains, and *Agropyron spicatum* and *Poa secunda* in the lower grassland zone in British Columbia[194] (Figures 1-14 and 1-15). Association of species may be brought about by the similarity in ecological amplitudes of two or more species; similarity in geographic ranges; differences in life-form (such as shallow and deep root systems) so that excessive competition can be avoided; dependence of one species upon another for shade (Figure 3-2), or for food as in parasites; or dependence for protection from grazing, as in grasses growing in dense clumps of cactus. Association may be so pronounced that a certain species may indicate the presence of other species in the stand, so that prediction is possible to some extent, i.e., if species *A* is found in a certain area then species *B* can also be expected there.

When environmental conditions change, the species that are associated will vary. A species growing as a dominant in one stand usually has different associates when growing as a subdominant in another stand; for example, *Agropyron spicatum* in western North Dakota, where it is near the eastern limits of its geographic range, is associated with *Muhlenbergia cuspidata, Carex filifolia, Bouteloua gracilis,* and *Eurotia lanata,* none of which grow with it in British Columbia where it is dominant. The presence or absence of certain associated species has important indicator value in pointing to significant conditions such as severe competition, presence of disease, or prevalence of one or more unfavorable environmental factors. Association of species is also important in testing new strains of forage plants, for usually they are grown in mixtures in meadows and pastures. Therefore the new strains need to be tested, not only in pure cultures to determine their suitability, but also in mixtures for their associative capacity.

A number of methods have been used to measure the degree of interspecific association.[95] The **association index,** one measure of ecologic association between plants, is secured by dividing the number (a) of random samples of a given stand in which species A occurs into the number (h) of samples in the same stand in which species A and B occur together. For example, if species A occurs in 40 sample areas ($a = 40$), and species B occurs together with A in 30 of these sample areas ($h = 30$), then the association index of species A is B/A, or 30/40, or 0.75; i.e., on three-fourths of the sample areas in which species A occurred it was associated with species B. But if species B is used as the base, the association index is 1.0. At least 100 samples should be taken for these calculations.

Another, probably more meaningful method uses the **index of similarity** of Sörensen,[62,103] which was developed originally on the basis of species presence. If a represents the total number of species in type A, b the number in type B, and there are c species present in both types, then the index of similarity $= 2c \times 100/a + b$. Instead of using the number of species, the index can be calculated on the basis of the average cover estimates or abundance. In this procedure a represents the sum of all averages of estimates of species found in vegetation type A, b the similar figure for type B, and c the sum of the various estimates of species shared by both types.

Population Density

Population density, broadly considered, denotes the number of individual plants or stalks in an area, but in a strict sense it refers to the number of individuals or stalks in a unit of space. When the measured unit area is divided by the number of individuals, the average area occupied by each individual is obtained. The number of individuals of a species varies from place to place in a stand, often considerably, so numerous sample areas are needed for reliable results. In range-management literature, "density" is often used incorrectly for "cover."

The term **population density,** when referring to animals, often conveys not merely the idea of the number of animals in a unit of space, but also their number in relation to the available quantity of a limiting requisite,[150] and this thought is generally implied when the term **density-dependent factor** or **density-governing factor** is used. An example of this factor in vegetation is a pine stand where the density of the trees reduces the light intensity so much that the number of trees reaching maturity is restricted (Figure 2-3). A **density-independent factor** or **nonreactive factor**[150] is one that has little or no effect on density (for example, the CO_2 content of the atmosphere), because it rarely if ever influences the number of plants in an area.

Density values are significant because they show the relative importance of each species in a stand when they are similar in life-form and size (Figure 2-5). However, where the plants are different, such as grasses, forbs, and dwarf-shrubs (Figure 3-1), density alone is insufficient for comparison, and data on other characteristics, especially cover (see p. 102), should then be considered. For instance, in studies on forest vegetation, the trunk diameter and height and spread of the crown are frequently measured in addition to numerical abundance. Moreover, it is often difficult, as in the case of mat plants, to determine density because the stalks grow very close together; therefore it is often more feasible as well as more precise to measure the area occupied by each species than to attempt to count the stalks. Because of difficulties in distinguishing separate, individual plants, particularly those that propagate by rhizomes or runners, or because of limitations in time, estimation scales are often used. In a 5-fold scale, 1 denotes that the individuals are very sparse; 2, sparse; 3, infrequent; 4, frequent to numerous; and 5, very numerous. Such a scale has greater value if the grades are based upon approximate numbers, for example, *S* denoting 1 to 4 stalks per square meter; *I*, 5 to 14; *F*, 15 to 29; *N*, 30 to 99; and *VN*, 100 stalks or more. Or a logarithmic scale may be used.

Data on population density are often indispensable in measuring the effects of reseeding, burning, spraying, and successional changes. An interesting example is a recent study[211] on the natural replacement of the chestnut (*Castanea dentata*) (Figure 1-24C) which has been destroyed by blight in the southern Appalachian region. In 2569 openings created by the death of the chestnuts, 5046 individual replacement trees were found. The most numerous were *Quercus prinus* which made up 17 per cent of the total; *Q. rubra*, 16 per cent; and *Acer rubrum*, 13 per cent. Species of *Quercus* made up a total of 41 per cent of all the replacements. In another example in southern Idaho it was shown that if *Bromus tectorum* can be reduced from about 570 to 50 plants per square foot for one season, competition will be sufficiently reduced so that perennial grasses such as bluebunch wheatgrass (*Agropyron spicatum*), crested wheatgrass (*A. cristatum*), and others will grow after seeding.[113]

The number of stalks that have been grazed compared to those not grazed have been used to determine the proper degree of utilization of the range. The effects of drought and subsequent recovery were measured by the number of stalks of common grasses in western North Dakota. In 1935 when the precipitation was about average, *Andropogon scoparius* had 874 stalks per square meter; in 1936, a drought year, 509 stalks; in 1937, 235 stalks; and in 1938, 303. Both 1937 and 1938 were nearly normal years. The number of stalks of *Agropyron smithii* for the same years were 140, 51, 69, and 98, respectively.[202A]

Cover (Area Occupied)

Cover, or specifically **herbage cover,** signifies primarily the area of ground occupied by the leaves, stems, and inflorescences, i.e., the above-ground parts of plants, as viewed from above. Each layer of vegetation is considered separately, since overlapping usually occurs, so that a tall plant is rated apart from one growing under it. **Basal area,** however, refers to the ground actually covered by the crown only, or actually penetrated by the stems, and readily seen when the leaves and stems are clipped at the ground surface. "Basal area" has also been used to denote the area occupied by the vegetation at 1 in., or at some other level, above the ground (Figures 1-20 and 1-21).

Discretion must be used in comparing cover data of various species which may have been taken at different heights, and often comparisons are not valid.[99] Measurements of basal area may vary considerably for the same plant, depending upon the height at which the measurements are taken (Figure 1-2). For example, in the same quadrat the area at the surface occupied by *Aristida longiseta* was 382 cm^2, and by *Buchloe dactyloides,* 408 cm^2; at a height of 1 in. the respective areas were 914 and 505 cm^2; and the total herbage covers of each were 1666 and 505 cm^2, respectively. The former grows in small bunches that have their maximum spread above 1 in., while the latter, a mat-former, often has its maximum spread below 1 in., so the last measurements present the most reliable comparison.[104] Under the influence of prevailing conditions herbage cover data are comparable, but it is often difficult to make valid comparisons of basal-area data of different life-forms even in the same sample area. It may be desirable in some studies, however, such as those on the effects of runoff, erosion, and grazing, to use basal area; but the measurements should then be taken of the maximum crown spread, which in bunchgrasses such as *Festuca arizonica* and *Muhlenbergia montana* may be at 3 to 5 in. above the ground, while in sodgrasses such as *Bouteloua gracilis* it is often less than 1 in. Decreases in runoff and erosion may often be correlated better with crown spread of bunchgrasses than with basal area.

In research on grasslands in which permanent effects of grazing are determined, charting or measurement of the vegetation is often made at a height of 1 in.—the height to which many species are grazed—and the data presented as basal area. The spread of herbage is influenced not only by the grazing of livestock, but also by attacks of insects, by fungi, and by weather conditions. Therefore, since basal area is more stable under such seasonal influences, although subject to long-continuing influences, its use as a means of measurement is preferred for many purposes.

Herbage area is one of the most important characteristics of vegetation in determining the nature of a community, such as quantitative relations between species. For example, the sand dune-sage type in the southern Great Plains was found to contain a total of 50 species of grasses and 216 species of forbs and shrubs. The average cover of all the vegetation was 34.3 per cent, which was divided among the following: *Artemisia filifolia,* 79.2; *Bouteloua gracilis,* 6.3; *Sporobolus cryptandrus,* 5.3; other perennial grasses, 2.4; annual grasses, 0.9; other shrubs, 4.9; and all forbs, 1.0 per cent.[175] A species may vary greatly in cover in various stands, as shown by *Vaccinium uliginosum* in Alaska, which varies in average herbage cover from about 22 per cent in stands where it is one of the dominants to 9 per cent or less where it is not a dominant.[100] Cover is often the most suitable expression for recording change (see Chart 4), but for single- or few-stalked plants, population density is a better characteristic to use.

Many methods have been used in securing data on cover, including (1) charting by hand or with a pantograph which is set up on a low table, (2) area listing, (3) point-contacts, and (4) line-interception; and various estimation methods such as (5) cover scales, (6) point-observation plot or square-foot density, and (7) ocular or range reconnaissance. The methods have been described in numerous publications and summarized and evaluated in a few.[99,27]

In Europe, sample areas to establish the relative importance of species in vegetation have been in use for more than a century. Sample areas for determining changes caused by grazing or induced by various kinds of management procedures, or to chart the course of succession following disturbance, may be established

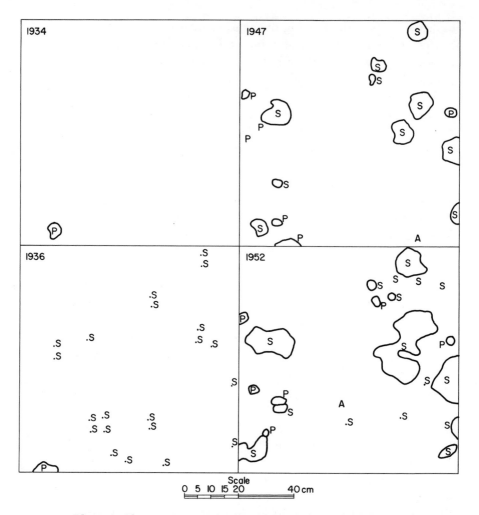

Chart 4. Changes in species composition and basal area on a permanent meter-square quadrat from 1934 to 1952 at the U. S. Sheep Experiment Station, near Dubois, Idaho, altitude 5500 ft. A letter symbol with no area mapped indicates plant cover of less than 0.5 cm². (A) *Agropyron spicatum;* (P) *Poa secunda;* (S) *Stipa comata;* (•) seedling. (After Blaisdell, J. P. (15A), "Seasonal Development and Yield of Native Plants on the Upper Snake River Plains and Their Relation to Certain Climatic Factors," Figure 9, *U. S. Dept. Agric. Tech. Bull.,* No. 1190, 1–68 (1958).)

permanently; or they may be set up temporarily for the purpose of ascertaining the present plant composition or other characteristics.

A stand may be sampled by a single, carefully located area, preferably starting at 10 m² and then enlarging it to 50 or 100 m² for a second look, as is commonly done in central Europe;[25] or it may be sampled by a number of small areas distributed throughout the stand, as is the usual practice in North America and Scandinavia. The size of the sample area to use depends upon the kind of vegetation that is being studied; in grasslands it is usually a square meter, in forests an area 10 meters square. For reliable results, a large number of sample areas should be used —the smaller the sample area the larger should be the number. In a grassland stand that is fairly homogeneous and not too large, 20 sample areas are usually adequate, while in a forest stand at least 10 should be used. The advantage of employing many small sample areas is that each stand can be studied very thoroughly, while the advantage in using one or a few large samples is the saving in time so that more stands can be investigated.

Height of Plants

The height of plants is usually a very good indicator of their condition or vigor, and, therefore, can be employed as a criterion of the success of a species in various habitats. It can also be used as a measure of the favorableness of the environment (Figure 1-11) and is much used by foresters as an index of site quality for various species of trees. Usually there is a good correlation, as high as 0.9 or even more, between the rate of growth in height and growth in weight; hence, growth curves are often based on height measurements instead of dry weights because of their convenience (see Chart 5).

It is somewhat difficult at times to secure accurate measurements because the height attained by the stems and leaves varies with individual plants of the same species growing under similar conditions. The approximate average height of the herbage in fairly dense stands can be secured by sighting along the top of the vegetation with a ruler, or the maximum and minimum heights of

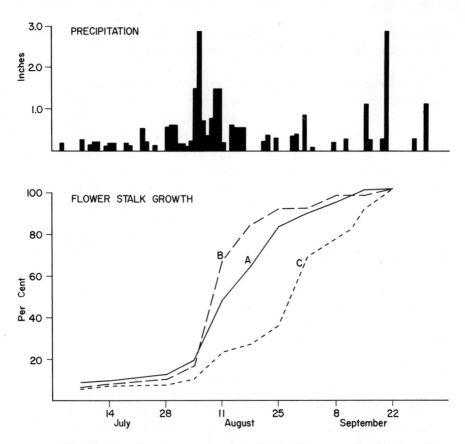

Chart 5. Growth curves as measured by height of flower stalks of (A) *Bouteloua filiformis*, (B) *Bouteloua rothrockii*, and (C) *Trichachne californica* in relation to the distribution of rainfall during one summer on the Santa Rita Experimental Range in Southern Arizona. (After Reynolds, H. G. (169A), "Managing Grass-Shrub Cattle Ranges in the Southwest," Figure 5, *U. S. Dept. Agric. Handbook,* No. 162, 1–40 (1959).)

a large number of individual plants can be measured. The plants measured in the field should be marked and numbered so that measurements can be taken of the same ones each time. Stems may also be cut at the ground level and taken to the laboratory for more accurate measurements.

Many interesting and important results have been gained by

height measurements, such as the effects of the competition of *Artemisia tridentata* upon 17 species of range grasses artificially seeded in northern Nevada. In early spring, *Agropyron cristatum* was only 4 in. tall under intense competition with *A. tridentata*, but 7 in. tall where the competition was lacking. The heights of *Agropyron smithii* were 15 and 17 in., respectively, showing that this grass resisted the competition better than the other *Agropyron*.[173]

The height of the herbage and the depth of the root system often show a relationship. For example, *Buchloe dactyloides* in Nebraska, with an herbage height of 5.5 in., had a **working depth** (the depth to which a large number of roots penetrate) and a maximum depth of the root system at 12 and 20 in., respectively; but when the herbage height was 3 in. the root depths were only 5 and 9 in., respectively. Another relationship was also noted: in six grass species the width of the third leaf from the ground varied in accord with the diameter of the roots at a depth of 6 in.[199]

In comparing the effects of systems of grazing upon the vegetation, flower stalks were cut at the close of the growing season and taken into the laboratory for making precise measurements. The average length of 100 stalks of *Agropyron smithii* from a deferred and rotation pasture in northern Colorado was 23.0 in. and that from an adjoining continuously grazed pasture, 18.7 in.; and the respective heights of *Stipa viridula* in the same habitats were 32.1 and 24.1 in.[105]

Height measurements are excellent for showing the effects of clipping species at various heights and frequencies. In eastern Montana *Bouteloua gracilis*, clipped during the growing seasons from 1938 to 1941, showed the following results in 1942 when it was not clipped: [111]

Height and Frequency of Clipping 1938 to 1941	Height of Seed Stalks in 1942, cm	Length of Basal Leaves in 1942, cm
2 cm every 2 weeks	23.7	11.2
2 cm every 4 weeks	24.1	13.1
4 cm every 2 weeks	26.6	15.4
Once at end of season	30.3	15.9

An important application of height measurements, especially on National Forest ranges, is the determination of range readiness in the spring. The proper height of the herbage for the beginning of grazing varies from 2 to 10 in. depending upon the growth habits of various species,[56] so when the chief forage plants reach their respective readiness heights, the grazing season is opened. Other criteria are also useful in this determination, such as the time of appearance of the first flowers of certain species. The height to which grasses are grazed is also commonly used as a measure of the proper degree of utilization of the range. For example, in southern Colorado the optimum utilization of Arizona fescue and mountain muhly is recommended as 35 to 40 per cent of the total growth. Therefore, the average height of the former at the end of the grazing season should be 5 to 6 in., and of the latter, a smaller bunchgrass, 1.5 to 2 in.[117]

Much research has been conducted to relate height measurements to the weight of forage for use in determining proper utilization of the range. Tables have been prepared to show the weight of each inch of height growth, and converting factors and graphs used to show the relation of height to weight, with scales for field work.[137] These investigations indicate that such methods are often useful. However, the research has shown the complexity of the interrelations between height and weight and, although the rates of growth in height and weight usually show a high correlation, it is more reliable to measure each one directly. The reason for this is that every characteristic of plants is governed by its own set of physiologic processes, and each set reacts to the environmental factors in its own particular way. The temptation is all too common in field work to reduce the number and kind of measurements in order to save time and avoid inconvenience, and to make inferences that are too broad and not warranted by the data.

Weight of Plants

Weight is one of the most important quantitative characteristics of plants, for an increase in dry weight is probably the best single measure of growth (Figure 3-3). Height and area of herbage are important space characteristics, while weight is the quantitative expression of the total mass of structural materials, food substances, protoplasm, and other substances that have resulted from the metabolic processes and form the basic reservoir of materials for additional growth and for the endurance of, and recovery from, unfavorable conditions. It is the total weight of these substances that constitutes the forage value of the herbage. Height and area are expressions of the distribution of the mass in space, and determine the availability of the herbage for grazing. Most of the research on weight has been done on the above-ground parts of plants, but in recent years some work has been done on the weight of root systems, and of leaves separately from the stems.

Clipping of the plants within sample areas to secure green or dry weights has been widely practiced for a long time. The plants may be clipped with grass shears, hand sickles, lawn mowers, field mowers, or plucking by hand to more closely resemble grazing, but even this may not yield data comparable to grazing because of the differentiating effects of the livestock. Sheep, especially, are highly selective in choosing plants or parts of plants. In order to protect vegetation from grazing, fenced plots and movable cages, varying from a few square feet to several square yards or more, are often employed. A commonly used size of cage covers 9.6 sq ft because the weight in grams from such a plot, multiplied by 10, equals the weight in pounds per acre. Cages may be located permanently, annually, or for shorter periods, depending upon the frequency and duration of the clipping operation. When only the total herbage yield is needed the procedure is rapid, but when the yield of each species is wanted, the separation of the plants of each kind, before or after clipping, is tedious and time-consuming, but the resulting data may be essential in solving some problems. Significant differences in botanical composition may occur between grazed and mowed stands because the latter may change more rapidly in species composition. To avoid many difficulties the sampling areas should be relocated at fairly frequent intervals.

As discussed under the section on height, estimation methods are used in determining yield or utilization by counting the number of stems that have been grazed on small plots and then estimating for each species the weight of the forage that has been eaten. Considerable training is required for using this method, but one advantage is that the actual weight of the yield of each species can be used in training and in checking the estimates. In grazing studies estimates of weight deserve wider use and may be more valuable than those of cover, for the percentage composition of species in an area usually varies with the characteristic that is measured. For example, in the same meter-square quadrat in northern Colorado, western wheatgrass comprised 9 per cent of the total basal area of all species but 31 per cent of the total actual weight of all species, and the corresponding figures for buffalograss were 45 and 8, respectively.[104] While the area of the latter was much greater, the grazing value of the former, as shown by the dry weight, was considerably higher.

The use of animals as instruments for measuring the grazing value of plants includes methods such as the weights of cattle or sheep, carrying capacity in numbers of animals, production of milk or beef, total digestible nutrients, digestion trials, palatability trials, and biological assays with small animals. Periodic weighing of animals, especially beef cattle, dairy heifers, or sheep, is less complicated than measuring the production of milk from dairy cows, but precautions must be taken to select highly similar animals. Special devices such as movable pens and tethering have been developed for using sheep in evaluating pastures. Some objections to the live-weight method are (1) the difficulty of control, (2) the relatively small areas grazed, and (3) the inexactness of comparing a grassland under a short-term experiment to one grazed for a long period under field conditions. The total digestible nutrient method is considered by many to be the best for evaluating pasturage when milk-producing cows are used. The nutrients supplied in the herbage and in supplementary feeds are considered in relation to the requirements of digestible nutrients for the milk production, maintenance of the animals, and for increases in live weight.[27]

The nature of the chemical components of plants is important in many ways, and considerable variation exists between and within species and at different times of the year. The quantity of organic food reserves in the basal parts of plants often determines the renewal of growth and the winter survival of many plants which have been subjected to adverse conditions. A plant may be rich in food substances, but because of the presence of some unpalatable material such as tannin in lespedeza or coumarin in sweet clover, it is not eaten. The stiffening and hardening of plants, caused chiefly by the formation of lignin in cell walls, proceeds rapidly as plants mature, resulting in decreased forage value. A number of plants growing in the western states absorb selenium from the soil and accumulate it in such concentrations as to cause poisoning of livestock that eat them. On the other hand, some substances are especially good indicators of the quality of forage. For example, routine analyses are made of the carotene content of hay to determine the best methods of drying. For increased accuracy, the part of the plant that is actually consumed should be analyzed rather than the entire plant, as exemplified by the leaves of clover and grass, which are eaten by sheep in preference to the stems.

Volume Occupied by Plants

Weight is a more important characteristic when plant growth or productivity is being considered, but the space occupied by the above-ground parts is of greater import in understanding the structure of the vegetation. The word "volume" has occasionally been used in place of weight, especially in dealing with the height-weight relations of range plants. The term "weight" refers to the heaviness property of matter, "volume" to the three-dimensional space occupied by an object. Except in forestry where the volume of trunks of trees is measured for the yield of lumber, little work has been done on volume, so it offers a productive field for research.

The volume of smaller plants may be determined by immersing them in water in a graduated vessel and measuring the displacement. An analysis in the USSR revealed that the total vol-

ume of 22 species of dicotyledons growing in an area of 0.25 m²
was 164 cc, while that of 6 monocotyledons in the same area was
65 cc—a ratio of 2.5 to 1,[1] but the ratio of numbers was 3.7 to 1.
The volume occupied by plants cannot be inferred from weight
measurements because the weight per unit of volume, the
density, varies for different parts of plants and for different
species; for example, clovers weigh more per unit of volume than
do grasses (Figure 1-15).

Frequency

Frequency is concerned with the degree of uniformity of the
occurrence of individuals of a species within an area. It is measured by noting the presence of a species in sample areas which
are distributed as widely as possible throughout the stand, the
results being expressed as a percentage, the **frequency index** or
percentage frequency. For example, if one or more individuals
of a species is found in each of 15 of a total of 25 samples, its frequency is 60 per cent.

The distribution of a species is rarely regular or uniform in a
stand (Figures 3-1 and 3-3). Variation is caused by many influences, such as microhabitat conditions of topography or soil
(Figure 2-4), vegetative propagation, quantity and dispersal of
seeds, time of invasion of one species as compared to others, grazing by livestock, activity of rodents, and depredation by insects
or diseases. As a result, patterns may be present, with centers of
higher frequency and greater abundance separated by areas of
lower frequency and abundance. A pattern of alternation or
interdigitation is more pronounced where the topography is
irregular or where the soil varies within short distances. For example, in an abandoned field in Louisiana the frequency of Johnson grass (*Sorgum halepense*) was 28 per cent in the old furrows and
0 per cent on the 6-in. higher ridges, and that of paspalum (*Paspalum conjugatum*) 4 per cent in the furrows and 22 per cent on
the ridges; while the dominant, goldenrod (*Solidago hirsutissima*),
was high in both—98 and 84 per cent, respectively.[160]

Frequency determinations by means of sample areas are often
needed in order to check general impressions about the relative

values of species in a stand, for conspicuous plants such as sunflowers or goldenrods may appear more widespread and abundant than they actually are in comparison to other species. Another good example is seen in Iowa prairies where the blazing star and prairie clover, with their extremely slender stems and leaves, have little cover value although the appearance of the prairie at certain seasons is caused by their high frequencies.[7]

Many species having low cover or population density also rate low in frequency, but some may have high frequency because of their uniform distribution. Usually, however, if the cover and population density are high the frequency will be high. In natural communities the individual plants or animals tend to aggregate because the offspring are more numerous near the parents or in the more favorable habitats than elsewhere; in other words, they are **clumped** (**over-dispersed,** showing **contagious distribution**) (Figures 1-27 and 2-4). Organisms under some conditions are **regularly spaced** (**under-dispersed**) such as grasses set out on a sand dune or plants in a corn field (Figure 1-3). When the plants or animals occur entirely by chance, as may happen in a small, uniform area, the distribution is **normal** or at **random.**[8,95]

Raunkiaer[169] was the first to use frequency extensively. He classified the occurrence of species in an area into five classes of frequency: A, 1 to 20 per cent; B, 21 to 40; C, 41 to 60; D, 61 to 80; and E, 81 to 100. On the basis of about 1350 frequency determinations in various types of communities in Denmark, the following distribution was found: A, 65 per cent of the total; B, 11; C, 7; D, 6; and E, 11. The classification of 8078 determinations by several investigators in various countries gave the following weighted average percentages: A, 53; B, 14; C, 9; D, 8; and E, 16. The normal distribution of the frequency percentages, derived from such classifications, is expressed as $A > B > C \gtreqless D < E$, and has been named Raunkiaer's "Law of Frequence." The ratio is the result largely of the effects of the dominant species which, by their superior competitive capacity, prevent others from equalling them in frequency; but they cannot prevent many species from invading some of the spaces.

The normal frequency ratio is useful in many kinds of studies in testing the uniformity of the vegetation, the most essential point being that class E should be larger than class D. This objective method can be quickly applied in the field, before proceeding with more detailed analysis. For example, in a representative stand of the *Stipa comata-Bouteloua gracilis-B. curtipendula* type in the lower foothills of Colorado, the number of species in 20-m² quadrats was A, 24; B, 6; C, 3; D, 2; and E, 5. In a nearby *Artemisia frigida*-weed stand on similar soil in a prairie-dog town the distribution was A, 10; B, 6; C, 4; D, 2; and E, 1, the difference between the two ratios indicating considerable disturbance.

The ratio may be affected by the intensity of grazing, as shown in an analysis of *Agropyron smithii* range land in Colorado where the ratio was 62, 14, 7, 7, and 10 in a deferred-rotation pasture to 59, 13, 13, 11, and 4 in an adjoining, continuously grazed pasture.[102] These ratios indicate that palatable species of low frequency tended to disappear under continuous grazing, while unpalatable species of low frequency tended to increase under the same conditions. This was exemplified by *Eurotia lanata,* a palatable shrub, which had a frequency of 56 per cent under deferred-rotation grazing but 0 per cent under continuous grazing, while the unpalatable *Artemisia frigida* on the other hand, had frequencies of 16 and 52, respectively, under the two grazing conditions. When the total number of species in a stand is small they often tend to be confined to classes A and E, and, obviously, in almost pure stands they are almost exclusively in class E. The number and size of sample areas influence the ratios; if too large or too small, the ratios tend to be obscured. The square meter has been widely employed in grassland research, so that data from many areas are comparable, but smaller sizes have also been extensively used.[95]

The frequency index has been employed to reveal differences between grasslands subjected to various conditions. The effects of grazing upon the frequency of prairie species in Missouri[71] are shown in the following table. The data indicate that competition between species, especially in the case of *Andropogon gerardi* in

	Grazed Prairie, %	Ungrazed Prairie, %
Andropogon gerardi	86	100
Andropogon scoparius	99	59
Sorghastrum nutans	98	57
Panicum lanuginosum		
var. fasciculatum	98	46
Poa pratensis	79	48
Carex hirsutella	98	21
Trifolium repens	49	13
Antennaria neglecta	99	13

the ungrazed prairie, was probably an important interaction.

Attempts have been made to integrate the characteristics of abundance and frequency in estimations and measurements; even such terms as "sparse," "frequent," "abundant," and others, usually include connotations of both dispersal and numerical abundance or cover. Objective methods have been devised for integrating quantitative data on abundance and frequency,[27] and the frequency-abundance index has been used to advantage in comparing the importance of one or more species in various communities.[106] This is exemplified in the following table showing ratings of five species in three communities in western North Dakota, on the basis of 100 as the maximum (Figure 2-6). These index figures were used as one of the chief criteria in classifying 36 stands into 9 community-types.

The frequency-abundance index was also used effectively in comparing a virgin grassland with two grazed grasslands in the

	Bouteloua-Stipa-Carex	Agropyron-Bouteloua-Carex	Andropogon scoparius
Bouteloua gracilis	100	100	3
Stipa comata	70	1	0
Agropyron smithii	8	100	3
Carex filifolia	28	97	23
Andropogon scoparius	0	0	100

Badlands of western North Dakota,[132] and some of the results are shown below.

	Virgin Grassland	Intermittently Used Grassland	Continuously Used Grassland
Bouteloua gracilis	47	66	100
Agropyron smithii	83	68	4
Stipa comata	14	25	2
Carex eleocharis and *C. pennsylvanica*	72	32	2

These figures, however, tend to obscure certain differences in the vegetation, for *Stipa* had the same frequency in the virgin and intermittently used grasslands, but the abundance was greater in the latter, thus making the index number higher in the latter. Integrated index figures are often useful, but they cannot replace the need for data on each characteristic separately.

The description of a stand requires the inclusion of data on frequency, which may be clearly shown in **stand tables,** such as Table 3-1. These tables are indispensable in depicting the composition of a stand for the kinds of species, and their cover values are listed according to groups such as shrubs or half-shrubs, grasses, forbs, mosses, and lichens. The tables also give a good idea of the pattern of distribution of all the species in the stand; for example, in Table 3-1 it is immediately noticed that *Loiseleuria procumbens* is not only the most abundant and dominant vascular plant, but that it occurs in clumps for the cover ranges from 1 to 4, while a lesser degree of aggregation occurs in the other species. On the whole this stand was fairly uniform because a number of species have average frequencies above 80 per cent—as indicated by the relative sparseness of blank spaces in the table. The table also shows the occurrence of bare ground in various parts of the stand, indicating the effect of adverse influences such as the activity of rodents or grazing and trampling by reindeer. It would have been desirable to give the cover of each species of lichen and moss separately, but time did not permit, and furthermore this would have been extremely difficult because of the large number of intergrown species in the 2-in.-thick layer.

TABLE 3-1. A *Loiseleuria procumbens-Cladonia* spp. STAND ABOUT 10 SQ. RODS IN AREA, 10 MILES EAST OF NOME, ALASKA. (On shallow soil consisting of dark brown loam to about 5 in., and mostly of loose, crumbling schist from 5 to 14 in. down. July 30, 1951.)

Species	(1)	(2)	(3)	(4)	(5)	(6)	(7)	(8)	(9)	(10)	Avg Cover	Frequency %
Loiseleuria procumbens	4	4	1	1	4	2	3	2	4	1	2.6	100
Empetrum nigrum		1	2	2		1	2	2	1	2	1.3	80
Betula nana exilis	1	1	1	1	2	2	1	1	1	3	1.4	100
Ledum decumbens	1	1	1	1	1	1	1	2	1	2	1.2	100
Vaccinium vitis-idaea	1	1	1	1	2	2	2	1	1	1	1.3	100
Vaccinium uliginosum	1		1	1			2	1		1	0.7	60
Salix pulchra								1			0.1	10
Salix phlebophylla		1									0.1	10
Carex montanensis	1	1	1	1	1	1	1	1	1	1	1.0	100
Hierochloe alpina	1		1	1	1	1	1	1	1	1	0.9	90
Pedicularis labradorica			1	1	1		1	1			0.5	50
Luzula multiflora							1			1	0.2	20
Festuca altaica										1	0.1	10
Luzula parviflora							1				0.1	10
Mosses	1	1	1	1	1	1	3	3	1	2	1.5	100
Lichens	6	3	6	6	6	6	5	6	5	6	5.5	100
Bare ground	1	3		1	1	1			1		0.8	60
No. of vascular spp. per m²	8	8	9	10	8	8	10	11	8	10		
Avg no. of vascular spp. per m²				9.0								

NOTE: Cover values are according to the Hult-Sernander scale: (1) herbage cover less than 1/16 of the m² sample area, (2) 1/16 to 1/8, (3) 1/8 to 1/4, (4) 1/4 to 1/2, (5) 1/2 to 3/4, (6) 3/4 to 4/4.[101] Additional vascular species present in the stand but not in any sample area are: *Arctagrostis alpina*, *Calamagrostis canadensis*, *Lycopodium annotinum*. Lichens: *Cladonia rangiferina*, *C. sylvatica*, *C. pleurota*, *C. cornuta cylindrica*, *C. macilenta squamigera*, *C. delessertii*, *Cetraria cucullata*, *Stereocaulon tomentosum*, *Pertusaria coccodes*, *Pilophorus cereolus*, *Thamnolia vermicularis*, and *Nephroma arcticum*. The more common mosses were *Polytrichum piliferum*, *Hylocomium splendens*, *Drepanocladus uncinatus*, *Ptilidium ciliare*, and *Bryum* sp. The moss-like *Selaginella selaginoides* was also common.[100]

Figure 3-4. The combination of several characteristics such as kinds of species, density, herbage cover, and height, make favorable habitats for wildlife; 10-day-old fawn of white-tail deer, near Hunt, Texas. May, 1959. (U.S.D.A. Soil Conservation Service.)

While there are important relations between frequency and population density, it appears that data on one can be transferred to the other only with the probability of considerable error, and, as in the relation of height to weight, it does not appear valid to transfer or interpret one in terms of the other. It is essential to measure each characteristic separately for truly quantitative data, although this requires more time for the field work (Figure 3-4).

The frequency index has proven very valuable in comparing different vegetation types, in determining the effects of various treatments or management practices and the role of microtopography in causing variations in the plant cover, and in evaluating the significance of species in various communities or at different times in the same community. For best results in vegetation analysis, the frequency index should be used in conjunction with other characteristics such as population density, cover, weight, height, periodicity, constancy, and fidelity. When time is limited for field work, frequency and cover are particularly serviceable in furnishing much information about the constituent species and about the nature of the stands.

SYNTHETIC CHARACTERISTICS OF THE COMMUNITY

Synthetic characteristics are generalizations or abstractions that are derived from data on analytic qualities, and integrate many of the analytic characteristics[99] which have been discussed in the previous chapter. They are:

(1) Presence and constancy
(2) Fidelity (Gesellschaftstreue)
(3) Dominance
(4) Physiognomy and pattern

During and following the analysis of a stand, the data on cover, numerical abundance, frequency, etc., are assembled in a stand table (see Table 3-1). After a number of stands have been analyzed, the tables are classified according to the community-types and the averaged or summarized data are assembled into a **synthesis** or **association table** (Table 4-1), so that ten or more stands are represented in a single table. Such tables of the various community-types in an area are indispensable in formulating information about the synthetic characteristics: presence and constancy, fidelity, dominance, physiognomy, and pattern.[24,25,11,166] In Table 4-1 are shown the approximately average

TABLE 4-1. A SYNTHESIS TABLE OF THE *Bouteloua gracilis-Artemisia dracunculus* ssp. *glauca* ASSOCIATION IN THE LOWER FOOTHILL REGION OF THE FRONT RANGE, COLORADO.[103] (Cover values are according to the Hult-Sernander scale as explained in Table 3-1.)

Stand number	(2)	(23)	(26)	(28)	(34)	Approx Avg Cover Value	Con- stancy
Date, 1953	7-24	8-3	8-3	8-4	8-5		
Area of sample, m²	16	22	20	20	16		
Slope, deg	S,0-5	W,15	SW,20	NE,1-2	W,10		
Cover, per cent	70	70	60	70	70		
Total number of species	18	21	22	20	27		
Agropyron smithii					1	0.2	20
Aristida longiseta	1	1	2	1	1	1.2	100
Bouteloua curtipendula	1	1	1	1	1	1.0	100
Bouteloua gracilis	5	5	4	5	4	4.6	100
Bouteloua hirsuta			1			0.2	20
Bromus japonicus	1	1	1	1	1	1.0	100
Bromus tectorum	1	1		1	1	0.8	80
Buchloe dactyloides					3	0.6	20
Carex heliophylla					1	0.2	20
Hordeum pusillum	1				1	0.4	40
Koeleria cristata					1	0.2	20
Schedonnardus paniculatus	1					0.2	20
Sitanion hystrix	1		1	1		0.6	60
Sporobolus cryptandrus		1				0.2	20
Stipa comata		1	2	2	1	1.2	80
Allium geyeri		1				0.2	20
Artemisia frigida	1	1	1	1	1	1.0	100
Artemisia d. glauca	1	2	2	2	2	1.8	100
Artemisia ludoviciana					1	0.2	20
Astragalus shortianus			1			0.2	20
Camelina microcarpa		1			1	0.4	40
Comandra pallida	1					0.2	20
Draba nemorosa			1	1		0.4	40
Eriogonum alatum					1	0.2	20
Eriogonum effusum		1	1			0.4	40
Euphorbia robusta		1				0.2	20
Evolvulus nuttallianus	1	1	1	1		0.8	80

Table 4-1 (Contin.)

Stand number	(2)	(23)	(26)	(28)	(34)	Approx Avg Cover Value	Con-stancy
Date, 1953	7-24	8-3	8-3	8-4	8-5		
Area of sample, m²	16	22	20	20	16		
Slope, deg	S,0-5	W,15	SW,20	NE,1-2	W,10		
Cover, per cent	70	70	60	70	70		
Total number of species	18	21	22	20	27		
Gaura coccinea	1	1	1	1	1	1.0	100
Gutierrezia sarothrae	1					0.1	20
Haplopappus spinulosus	1	1	1			0.6	60
Helianthus petiolaris					1	0.2	20
Helianthus pumilus	1			1		0.4	40
Liatris punctata				1		0.2	20
Lithospermum incisum			1	1		0.4	40
Mertensia lanceolata		1				0.2	20
Mirabilis linearis				1		0.2	20
Oenothera brachycarpa		1				0.2	20
Oxytropis lambertii			1			0.2	20
Psoralea tenuiflora	1	1	1	1	1	1.0	100
Ratibida columnifera					1	0.2	20
Scutellaria brittonii					1	0.2	20
Senecio fendleri					1	0.2	20
Sphaeralcea coccinea	1	1	1	1	1	1.0	100
Thelesperma megapotamicum				1		0.2	20
Tragia urticifolia		1				0.2	20
Viola nuttallii					1	0.2	20
Neobesseya missouriensis			1		1	0.4	40
Opuntia polyacantha				1	1	0.4	40
Opuntia rafinesquei			1			0.2	20
Cladonia pyxidata pocillum					1	0.2	20
Nostoc sp.		1				0.2	20

cover values of the species within a single large sample in each of five different stands in the *Bouteloua gracilis-Artemisia dracunculus* spp. *glauca* community-type. The table reveals at once that only a few species are generally prevalent throughout the five stands, and still fewer provide much herbage cover, all this giving a fairly good representation of this community-type. The large number of gaps in the table indicate the scattered and sparse occurrence of most of the species.

The soils (Brown Soils group) in these stands contained a moderate number of gravel particles and rocks both on the surface and to a depth of 18 in. Between the surface and 12 in. the sandy clay loam was dark reddish-brown to red; between 12 and 18 in. the soil varied from sandy clay loam to clay loam, reddish-brown to weak red in color; the lime content was usually high throughout and the pH was 8.0 to 8.2.

Presence and Constancy

As stated in Chapter 3, frequency refers to the degree of uniformity of distribution of a species within one stand; presence and constancy refer to how uniformly a species occurs in a number of stands of the same type of community, for example, when a species is found in 18 of 20 stands in one community type the presence or constancy is 90 per cent. The term **constancy** is employed when equal, measured sample areas are used in each stand, **presence** is used when the area of the sampling unit varies from stand to stand, and especially when it is not measured. It is preferable, when possible, to use measured units so comparisons can be made more readily, and for possible statistical analysis. Often, however, the sampling units cannot have the same area because of the nature of the vegetation, as, for example, small irregular stands in rock crevices or on sand deposits along a stream. When a single sampling unit per stand is employed, it should be large enough to include most of the species in the stand. This is called the **minimal area,** which is determined by using the species number:area curve, the number being represented on the ordinates axis, the area on the abscissas. The point where the curve begins to flatten denotes approximately the minimal area, which may vary from less than 10, to 25 sq m or more in various kinds of vegetation. Whenever possible, at least ten stands should be analyzed for each kind of community.

Species may be classified into five classes of constancy according to the percentage of stands in which they occur, as follows:

Species are present
  I. In less than 20 per cent of the stands
 II. In 21 to 40 per cent
III. In 41 to 60 per cent
 IV. In 61 to 80 per cent   .
  V. In 81 to 100 per cent

A fairly large number of species in classes IV and V indicates floristic homogeneity in the community-type;[25] for example, in the type represented in Table 4-1, the distribution is: I, 29; II, 8; III, 2; IV, 3; and V, 9. (All of the species with a constancy of 20 were placed in class I because of the small number of stands.) A high degree of constancy indicates that a species has wide ecological amplitude and is therefore capable of growing in various microhabitats, or that the various stands occur in sites that are very similar in environmental conditions so that species of narrow amplitude can grow in all of them.

Species that occur in 90 per cent or more of the stands in Central Europe, or in over 80 per cent in Scandinavia, are called **constant species,** and those with high cover values or numerical abundance are usually good competitors and often dominants. These species are important in characterizing and distinguishing community-types,[101,103] as indicated by the lists of constants in two community-types in the lower foothills of Colorado, shown below:

Bouteloua gracilis-Artemisia d. glauca community	*Andropogon* community
Bouteloua gracilis (dominant)	*Andropogon scoparius* (dominant)
Artemisia d. glauca (dominant)	*Andropogon gerardi*
Bouteloua curtipendula	*Bouteloua curtipendula*
Aristida longiseta	*Bouteloua gracilis*
Bromus japonicus	*Koeleria cristata*
Artemisia frigida	*Stipa comata*
Gaura coccinea	*Artemisia frigida*
Psoralea tenuiflora	*Psoralea tenuiflora*
Sphaeralcea coccinea	*Artemisia ludoviciana*
	Paronychia jamesii

Similarity or "relationship" increases between community-types as the number of constant species present in common becomes greater, so they form an important criterion in the classification of the types (associations, sociations) into higher categories (alliances), which is discussed further in Chapter 6.[11]

Fidelity

Fidelity refers to the degree that a species is restricted in its occurrence to a particular kind of community (Figures 1-27 and 2-4); those with low fidelity occur in a number of different communities, those with high fidelity in a few or in only one kind. This is because species differ in ecological amplitude or in capacity to grow in a wide range of ecological conditions, or because some species are able to associate with others or are prevented from doing so because of inability to compete. Other causes are dissimilarities in adaptations for migration and invasion, and also may be found in the history of geographical dispersal, including extinction of a species in local areas. Fidelity and constancy are independent characteristics, fidelity being concerned with the occurrence of a species in different kinds of community-types, constancy with various stands in the same kind of community-type. Fidelity can be determined only by analyzing stands in several to many types within a region, constancy by the analysis of several stands in the same community-type.

Five grades or classes of fidelity are used in the Braun-Blanquet scheme of classification,[25,11] as follows:

   (A) Characteristic species (character, faithful species[166])

      (5) Exclusive (treu), completely or almost completely restricted to one kind of community

      (4) Selective (feste), occurring most frequently in one kind of community, but also, though rarely, in other kinds

      (3) Preferential (holde), occurring more or less abundantly in several kinds of communities but with optimum conditions for abundance and vitality in one certain kind of community

(B) Companion species

    (2) Indifferent (vage), occurring without pronounced affinity or preference for any particular kind of community

(C) Accidental species

    (1) Strange (fremde), rare and accidental intruders from another community or relics from an earlier stage of succession.

The characteristic species, including the exclusive, selective, and preferential, together with those high in constancy, including the dominants, are the most important in characterizing a community-type. The greater the ratio of the total number of constant species to the total number in a particular community, the more developed is its homogeneity; and a large number of characteristic species makes the floristic delineation of a type sharper than a few. Community-types which have high ratios of both constant and characteristic species are well established, and consequently are unlikely to occur in newly formed habitats or in early stages of succession. Species of high fidelity may have considerable value in indicating ecological conditions, e.g., the restriction of certain species to particular soil conditions, but fidelity is primarily a sociological quality and **indicator species** is a more appropriate term for plants that are associated with such conditions. Some plant sociologists consider a high degree of constancy and dominance as more important than fidelity in characterizing communities;[166,151] however, for completeness in characterization both constancy and fidelity should be used as much as possible, for one complements the other.

    A few examples indicating the importance of fidelity will be given. In Iowa, some rather rare species of high fidelity are the first to disappear when the prairie is disturbed, and they also encounter great difficulty in becoming re-established; therefore, such plants are particularly important in describing highly developed prairie. In attempting re-establishment, a grouping of appropriate grasses might be considered satisfactory, but a genuine prairie must also contain the high-fidelity, exclusive species. For example, ground plum (*Astragalus crassicarpus*), prairie violet (*Viola pedatifida*), rough pennyroyal (*Hedeoma hispida*), and lousewort (*Pedicularis canadensis*) are all fairly common on upland prairie in Iowa; but the first two are the most exclusive. The other two rate much lower in fidelity, *Hedeoma* growing readily as a weed in dry soil, and *Pedicularis* occurring in woodlands farther eastward.[7] In western North Dakota, *Andropogon gerardi* and *Stipa spartea* were restricted to one of nine types of vegetation, thus rating in class 4; *Distichlis stricta* was restricted to two types, and so rated in class 3; *Bouteloua gracilis* and *Agropyron smithii* grew in all the types present, but having greatest abundance and vitality in only one type, they also rated in class 3.[106] A species growing near the limits of its geographical range, such as *Andropogon gerardi* and *Stipa spartea* in western North Dakota, can be expected to occur in fewer kinds of communities than when it is growing near the center (Figure 2-6).

Dominance

Dominance is the characteristic of vegetation which expresses the predominating influence of one or more species in a stand so that populations of other species are more or less suppressed or reduced in number or vitality. Dominants are those species which are so highly successful ecologically in their relations to the environment and with other species that they determine to a considerable extent the conditions under which associated species must grow. In a mature grassland (Figure 3-3), dominant species are few, in tropical rain forest, many. Cover and population density are the chief qualities determining dominance, but frequency, height, life-form, and vitality are also important. Height alone is insufficient, e.g., the tall goldenrods and asters in the prairie are not sufficiently numerous nor are the root systems well enough adapted to enable them to dominate the densely growing grasses. In savanna (Figure 1-12) the scattered trees or tall shrubs may be considered as physiognomic dominants together with the grasses, but the ecologic dominants are the grasses, for they exert more influence on the habitat and on other plants.

Figure 4-1. Big bluestem (*Andropogon gerardi*), one of the chief dominants in the tallgrass prairie, is a most successful grass because of its numerous well-adapted qualities. (U.S.D.A. Soil Conservation Service.)

When shrubs or trees such as mesquite or juniper grow closely enough together to form a canopy they become dominants in the uppermost layer, while the grasses are usually dominants in the ground layer.

The synthetic tables in which kinds of species, population density or cover, and frequency are shown furnish an excellent aid in the quantitative determination of dominants (Tables 3-1 and 4-1). The constants (species occurring in more than 80 per cent of the stands) with the highest cover or numerical abundance may be designated as dominants. Each layer is considered as having its own dominants—a common practice, especially in Scandinavia.[151,62] An example may be given from northern Colorado.[101] The *Stipa-Bouteloua* type *Stipa comata*, with an average cover of about 25 per cent and a constancy of 11.0 per cent, was the chief dominant, growing in the uppermost layer, while the other dominants, *Bouteloua gracilis* and *B. curtipendula*, with about 10 per cent in cover and 100 per cent in constancy, were in a lower layer. Most of the other species covered less than about 3 per cent, although the frequency of some was high.

Most of the analytical qualities, however, play a part in determining dominance. An excellent example is *Andropogon gerardi* which, for many reasons, is the most important dominant in broad lowland valleys in the tallgrass prairie region of the United States (Figure 4-1). It forms the topmost layer of herbage, has a deep and dense root system, tillers early, and has a long growing season. It also possesses excellent vigor, sod life-form, and a high degree of sociability; it forms almost complete foliage cover, has good ground cover, has a frequency index of 100 per cent, and produces a large yield in dry weight of from 400 to 725 g per sq m. Another outstanding dominant, occurring in pastures, is orchardgrass, which owes its success to excellent vitality, rapid growth of roots and shoots which starts early in the spring, a widely spreading and deeply penetrating root system, large crowns and good herbage cover, high frequency, and dense bunches. The annual, *Bromus tectorum*, apparently first noticed in the United States around the year 1900, has become dominant on millions of acres of the western range because of its large seed production, rapid germination and growth of shoots and roots when conditions are favorable, early maturity, and adjustment to drought and other unfavorable conditions such as overgrazing.

Physiognomy and Pattern

Physiognomy, the appearance or "look" of a stand, may be considered a synthetic quality because the appearance of vegetation is based on a number of qualitative and quantitative characteristics such as the kinds and dominance of species, life-form, population density, cover, height, sociability, stratification, association of species, and color. For example, the sod-like blue gramagrass-buffalograss type on the Great Plains differs strikingly in physiognomy from the little bluestem-bunchgrass type—in life-form, in the area of ground left bare, in height, in number of species, and in stratification. Another example is seen in western wheatgrass and cheatgrass which form stands of single- or few-stalked plants growing close together with a high degree of uniformity, very different from the clumped bluebunch-wheatgrass stands.

Physiognomy, although useful in recognizing and delineating different kinds of communities, cannot be substituted for analytic characters in sociological analysis, but it is valuable in preliminary investigations or reconnaissance, both on the ground and by airplane, to be followed by sociological analysis. Physiognomy is also useful in broad and general descriptions of vegetation as an introduction to thorough understanding of a stand. Complete sociological analyses, accompanied by physiognomic descriptions, are still needed for most vegetation types in North America.

Pattern in vegetation occurs in the form of groups or clumps of individuals, or in any other nonrandom arrangement of plants.[95] Physiognomic contrast between groups, such as shrubs in a grassland (Figure 1-8), or zones around a lake, accentuates pattern and is readily seen; but slight differences in density, cover, or frequency often require quantitative methods of determination before the pattern is detected. If the pattern is small in scale, sampling with a small quadrat is necessary to determine it, but if the pattern is both large in scale and high in intensity, such as patches of dense aggregations of individuals of a species separated by areas where they are absent, a large quadrat is needed. If, however, the pattern is large in scale but consisting, for example, of patches of one or more species of higher and lower density in a mosaic, a much smaller quadrat size is required. In analyzing vegetation for pattern, the qualities, density, cover, and frequency are most serviceable criterions.

Causes of pattern may be grouped under three headings: (1) morphological, in which the growth of a propagative organ such as a rhizome is very important; (2) sociological, in which competition and association of species are of great import; and (3) physiographic (Figure 1-4), in which topographic variations in soil moisture, concentration of nutrients, soil texture and structure, and others, are concerned.[125,126] In the initial colonization of an area (Figure 2-2) the distribution of a species may be at random and without noticeable pattern unless some spots are more favorable for growth than others, but contagious aggregation soon appears and results in morphological and physiographic patterns; following this, competition, replacement of species, and association of species lead to sociologic patterns. However, as the climax is approached the pattern becomes less pronounced, but even in the climax the three kinds of pattern usually exist.

GENERAL REFERENCES

Becking, R. W., "The Zürich-Montpellier School of Phytosociology," *Botan. Rev.,* **23,** 411–488 (1957).

Braun-Blanquet, J., "Plant Sociology," McGraw-Hill Book Co., New York, N.Y., 1932.

Braun-Blanquet, J., "Pflanzensoziologie. Grundzüge der Vegetationskunde," 2nd Ed., Springer-Verlag, Vienna, 1951.

Cain, S. A. and Castro, G. M. de O., "Manual of Vegetation Analysis," Harper & Bros., New York, N.Y., 1959.

Greig-Smith, P., "Quantitative Plant Ecology," Academic Press, Inc., New York, N.Y., 1957.

Hanson, Herbert C., "Ecology of the Grassland, II," *Botan. Rev.,* **16,** 283–360 (1950).

PART THREE

Dynamics of Communities

5

HABITAT PATTERNS, CHANGES, AND CLIMAX

An important feature of vegetation is change. Within a growing season the aspect of a community changes from spring to autumn because of differences in the requirements and ecological amplitudes of the various constituent species, some growing rapidly and flowering early, others developing more slowly. The beginning of growth, flowering, and fruiting of the same kind of plant comes at different times from year to year because the environmental conditions, particularly temperature and precipitation, vary. On account of drought, disease, and other adverse factors, or old age, some plants may fail to produce seed, or even die, and the space they occupied may be taken by other species the following year. Even the plants themselves, such as a dense stand of pines, modify the environment, especially by reducing the light intensity so that they cannot reproduce, and consequently, in time, they are replaced by deciduous trees.

Some types of vegetation at first appear uniform over large areas, but close examination reveals variation from place to place because the topographic and soil conditions change. Communities may be confined to relatively small areas because of the alterations in the environment, as is readily noted when one ascends a mountain or proceeds from a marshy lake shore to high land. The environmental conditions may change gradually in space, with corresponding alteration in the plant cover, forming a **cline,** or the change may be abrupt so that **sharp transitions** or discontinuities are produced.

It is evident that there are many kinds of change that occur in vegetation both in time in one place and in space from one area to another, and that they are related to alterations in environmental factors. These changes may be classified in three main groups. The first includes **changes in time** in a specific community that are **directional** with respect to loss of some of the present species and the invasion of new ones, with accompanying increase in complexity, as in **ecologic succession** where the directional change is from the less complex and less stable vegetation to the more complex and more stable, culminating in the climax or steady-state, while **retrogression** is the reverse of this. The second group includes **nondirectional** changes which occur over a period of time within one community, and may be **cyclic** or **noncyclic replacement,** and **fluctuations;** or the changes may involve several communities in one area, forming another kind of cyclic replacement. The third main group consists of changes in **space,** i.e., from area to area, such as gradual or sharp transitions in vegetation-types, among which are vertical and horizontal transitions, clines, and discontinuities. The treatment in the following pages will be in accordance with these concepts.

Another classification of time changes was proposed by Iaroshenko[113A] and described by Major.[142] In any natural vegetation these may occur at five definable levels: (1) seasonal, as seen in aspection; (2) annual or cyclic—related to variations in climatic or biotic factors; (3) successional; (4) historical—migration or extinction in relation to long-term climatic change; and (5) genetic—the evolution of a new flora.

One of the important and difficult tasks of the student of vegetation is to determine as fully as possible the status of each plant community with reference to the series of changes that have been, and are, taking place. In addition to sociological analysis, a complete description of vegetation must include discussion of the dynamics within and between communities, with particular reference to their position as a successional stage or a climax.

ENVIRONMENTAL GRADIENTS AND HABITAT PATTERNS

The **habitat** is the place occupied by a population or a community in which a particular combination of environmental conditions is present, such as the foothill slopes where ponderosa pines are growing, or a marshy lakeshore covered with sedges and associated species. The environmental conditions within one kind of habitat exhibit variation from spot to spot, either irregularly and suddenly, or gradually, as may be seen in going from a lakeshore inland. The extent of a habitat is delimited by the ecological amplitude of one or more of the species under consideration; for example, the habitat where *Pinus ponderosa* is dominant comprises the rocky foothills in many of the western states, varying considerably in altitude and latitude, with fairly wide ranges in precipitation, temperature, and other factors, each of which may change at a different rate than the others. For example, the temperature conditions may vary appreciably in an altitudinal range of 2000 feet, while the soil texture and humus content remain about the same. Major and minor habitats occur, the former marked by dominants in the vegetation, the latter by minor species associated with the dominants but requiring special conditions for their growth, such as mosses and lichens in openings among shrubs in the Subarctic, or between bunches of grass in prairie.

Since climatic, topographic, edaphic (soil), and biotic conditions vary to a greater or lesser degree within a landscape (see Figures 1-1 and 5-1), numerous habitats and plant communities are formed and become manifest in a mosaic or zonation of vegetation. The changes in vegetation are often more abrupt than those in habitat conditions, because when the ecological amplitude or requirements of one or more species, especially dominants,

Figure 5-1. Bare areas are formed in this region of pronounced changes by erosion, deposition, melting of glaciers,
and other factors. Note dense forest on lower slopes. Tracy
Arm, Alaska. (U. S. Forest Service.)

are surpassed, other species take over and competition between
species tends to produce sharper boundaries in communities than
occur in habitat conditions.[153] The transition from one type of
community to another may be gradual, especially where the
gradient changes slightly with distance, but the transition may
be sharp where discontinuities[205] in the environment occur, such
as considerable differences in the substratum which favor the
formation of discrete vegetation units.

Types of Gradients and Their Relations to Vegetation

In a given region a number of gradients are found, and within
each of them secondary gradients occur; for example, local
gradients are present on hillsides within the gradual gradient of

increasing elevation from Point Barrow to the Brooks Range in Alaska. Some gradients are on a large scale, such as this one in Alaska, and may be divided into sections. The major gradient in Spitzbergen, climatic in nature, was divided into four parts, based on the kinds and relative abundance of species, namely the barren, *Dryas, Cassiope,* and *Empetrum* zones. This gradient also is found, on a broader scale, in the Spitzbergen Archipelago, Greenland, arctic Canada, and in the mountains of Scandinavia.[187]

Gradients may occur on a medium scale, such as those formed in small mountain valleys in arctic and subarctic regions where snow accumulates during the winter. From the bottom of the valleys to the tops of the ridges changes occur in the depth and time of melting of the snow cover (see Charts 1 and 2, pp. 18 and 19), in the exposure to wind, especially in winter, and in insolation, temperature, availability of water, and solifluction.[151]

Gradients ("microgradients," "intrastand gradients," "microcommunity gradients") are also present within very small areas. These may be caused by variations in microrelief, in texture or organic content of the soil, in flow of surface water, or in other conditions; and are especially evident in the Arctic and Subarctic in frost scars, polygons, peat rings, stone stripes, tundra mounds, and solifluction terraces. An example will be given from Norwegian Lapland where five distinct kinds of habitats and vegetation types or phases occur within an area of a few square meters on dolomite slopes.[52] The first phase is characterized by barren, shallow mineral soil, occupied by many plants that are intolerant of competition, such as *Draba incana, Dryas octopetala, Festuca ovina,* and *Saxifraga oppositifolia.* Peat begins to accumulate, making possible the invasion of plants requiring a more organic substratum—the second phase. The vegetation then becomes closed and comprises the dominants *Carex rupestris* and *Dryas octopetala,* with *Arctostaphylos alpina* and *A. uva-ursi* prominent in the secondary group. The third phase, with deeper peat, has *Empetrum hermaphroditum* and *Vaccinium uliginosum* as dominants; and in the fourth phase, where considerable decomposed organic matter is present, lichens, especially *Cladonia* spp., are prominent. Erosion apparently begins and continues through the fifth phase, resulting in degradation to the mineral soil and renewal of the cycle.

The rate of change in space of one or more factors may be very gradual and take place over an extensive area, or it may be abrupt and very limited in extent. The rate of change usually varies throughout the gradient, rather than being uniform, because of the variability in topography, soils, and other conditions. The mixed prairie in western Nebraska and Kansas has been interpreted as a broad continuum between the tallgrass prairie and the shortgrass vegetation of the Great Plains, resulting from an elongated gradual gradient. Where the change is abrupt, either a discontinuity or a narrow transition belt is found, as, for example, on steep mountain slopes where a series of sharp changes occur (see Figure 5-1), or along seacoasts where salinity and soil moisture may favor distinct zones.

Relatively rapid changes in time of one or more environmental factors may occur which are unidirectional rather than fluctuational in nature. There may be a gradual decrease in the availability of soil moisture, as in the hydrosere, and this may occur along the entire gradient or at various rates in different portions. Where such a unidirectional change in gradient occurs there is an associated directional change, or succession, in communities on the same area; for example the cattail-reed stage is replaced by sedge-marsh, which in turn may be succeeded by a shrub stage—the first of these probably showing a more rapid decrease in soil moisture than the others. In time unidirectional changes slow down or terminate, and a more or less steady-state environmental complex, with a complex of climax communities, prevails.

Vegetation is an indicator of considerable reliability of the gradients of the environment. In the southern Appalachians it has been shown that the populations of a number of species and communities are related to the complex pattern of environmental gradients.[203,204,206] Each factor has a pattern of gradients which is related to those of other factors, so that a great complex of intergrading habitats results, accompanied by a very complex arrangement of communities.

The differences, therefore, in gradients in a landscape, many of them caused by microrelief, are important in defining community boundaries which may be sharp or clear-cut, transitional or diffuse, and mosaic-insular.[153] It appears that in some regions the vegetation may be a complex continuum of populations which are adjusted to the intricate pattern of environmental gradients.[60] However, because of the competition between species differing in capacity to utilize the environmental resources, communities are often more sharply delimited than the habitats. An example of the resulting complexity in vegetation is seen in the Cairngorm Mountains in Great Britain, well described by Metcalfe[147] as follows: "The result in toto is a vegetational patchwork related to local physiognomy, the units of which repeat over the whole area as the physiognomic features repeat, and in which the units can be differentiated from each other, not only by the presence or absence of the more sensitive or dependent species but also by the relative abundance and cover of the more tolerant and independent species." Even the smallest and poorest communities, containing only the most common species, indicate the ecologic conditions of their habitats by variation in quantitative composition. Mosses and lichens, lacking root systems, are especially sensitive indicators of moisture conditions.[78]

In summary, several to many environmental factors are functionally decisive in every area. Each environmental factor is usually characterized by macro-, meso-, and microgradients, the smaller ones being part of the larger. The gradients may be continuous or discontinuous, and they are generally variable rather than uniform throughout their extent. In some cases a portion or all of a certain gradient may change with time. Each factor tends to be operative within a limited range of independence of others. Intergradation of the gradients of all factors results in a complex pattern of habitats in every region. A nongradient environment probably never exists, even if a peneplain should develop by geomorphic processes. Populations and communities are in dynamic adjustment to the intergrading steady-state habitats, and also to changing habitats if they are present, so that a complex pattern of climax and successional vegetation types results. The communities tend to be more discrete than the habitats.

Replacement Change

Replacement change within a community is the loss of individuals which have died from other than catastrophic causes such as a forest fire, and the growth in their place of individuals which are usually of the same community. There are two types of replacement change, noncyclic and cyclic; they are operative within the other types of changes to be discussed, and they are not in opposition to them.

Noncyclic replacement may be considered as a normal replacement. When an individual of a given species dies, it will usually be replaced by an individual of a species which is a member of the respective community, but not necessarily of the same species. The death of the chestnut tree (*Castanea dentata*) has been gradual in the deciduous forest of the Great Smoky Mountains,[211] with swamp chestnut oak (*Quercus prinus*), red oak (*Q. rubra*), and red maple (*Acer rubrum*) as the most common replacement species growing in the openings.

This kind of change is on an individual basis. It need not be on a one-to-one basis, but certainly over a period of time it will tend to develop on this basis. It is rather obvious that, if a large dominant plant such as a mature tree dies, initially seedlings of several species will appear, but in due time a single dominant will survive, and the rate of replacement is dependent upon the life-spans of the respective species. There usually is neither a perceptible nor a significant change in composition or abundance of the dominant and characteristic species within a climax or a long-persisting stand, therefore a continuation of this process throughout the stand results in no significant change in its physiognomic character; however, in the case of the chestnut the floristic change is very significant. It is logical to assume that replacement change is operative within any community which persists for a time in excess of the life-spans of the dominant and characteristic species.

A cyclic replacement change is significantly different from the one previously discussed. A phasic cycle is a series of vegetation

and habitat changes that may be called a cyclic system, probably first described in detail by Watt.[197] He was particularly in-
terested in determining how the community maintains and re-
generates itself. In each of the seven communities that he

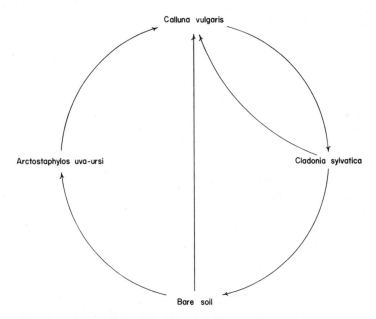

Chart 6. A cyclic system on the dwarf *Calluna vulgaris* community in the
Cairngorms, Scotland. (After Watt, A. S. (197), "Pattern and Process in the
Plant Community," Figure 2, *Jour. Ecol.*, 35, 1–22 (1947).)

described, the different kinds of patches are related to one another, and there is orderliness in the changes in an upgrade series
and in a downgrade series. One of these is the dwarf Callunetum
community in the Cairngorms (see Chart 6). *Calluna vulgaris* is at
the peak of the upgrade series, and after its death in a patch
Cladonia silvatica becomes dominant on the *Calluna* stems if protected, otherwise *Cladonia* is present but not dominant. Then
Cladonia disintegrates, and bare soil is exposed, with some remaining *Calluna* stems, terminating the downgrade series. *Arctostaphylos uva-ursi* initiates the upgrade series by invading the bare
area and completely occupying it. Then *Calluna* invades the

Arctostaphylos and becomes dominant, completing the upgrade series and one cycle. There are environmental gradient changes associated with each phase. In reality the phasic cycle in the dwarf Callunetum may consist of four, three, or two phases. The three-phase cycle consists of the usual *Calluna* phase, a downgrade series to the *Cladonia* and the bare soil phases, and then the upgrade series to the *Calluna* phase, without that of the *Arctostaphylos*. The two-phase cycle consists of the *Calluna* phase, a downgrade change to the *Cladonia* one, and then an upgrade change to the *Calluna* phase again to complete the cycle.

A cyclic change system occurs in patchy grassland in western North Dakota. In many areas there is a pattern of pitted patches which are bare or covered with a thin stand of weeds and low shrubs or grasses. The normal soil has a cover of blue gramagrass (*Bouteloua gracilis*), needle-and-thread (*Stipa comata*), sedges (*Carex filifolia, C. stenophylla*), and western wheatgrass (*Agropyron smithii*).[106,123] In the downgrade series, in the first stage, a saline soil (solonchalk) is developed by an excessive concentration of soluble salts in the upper layers. In the next stage, with an improvement in drainage, excess soluble salts are removed and an alkali soil (solonetz) develops. Then a soloth is developed which has a reduced ion exchange capacity, the A_2 horizon may be washed or blown away, and the vegetation is destroyed. *Bouteloua gracilis* usually persists as a dominant through the saline and alkali stages. In the saline stage, if the salts become too concentrated, *B. gracilis* may be replaced as a dominant by *Agropyron smithii*, desert saltgrass (*Distichlis stricta*) or alkaligrass (*Puccinella nuttalliana*), depending upon the concentration of the salt.

The significant processes in the development of normal soil in the upgrade series are calcification and reduction of sodium. The vegetation stages of the upgrade series are the forb and low-shrub stages, first grass stage, second grass stage, and the final stage; distinctive soil characteristics are associated with each upgrade stage. In the forb and low-shrub stages the exposed B_2 horizon is most commonly invaded by knotweed (*Polygonum erectum*), pepperweed (*Lepidium densiflorum*), the salt bushes (*Atriplex nuttallii* and *A. argentea*), plantain (*Plantago elongata*), prickly pear (*Opuntia frag-*

ilis), *Iva axillaris*, glasswort (*Salicornia herbacea*), desert saltgrass, broom snakeweed (*Gutierrezia saraothrae*), gum weed (*Grindelia squarrose*), *Suaeda depressa*, Russian thistle (*Salsola kali*), *Agropyron smithii*, and *Eriogonum multiceps*. The first grass stage is characterized by perennial grasses, the more important being wheatgrasses (*Agropyron molle, A. albicans, A. smithii*), *Puccinellia nuttalliana*, tumblegrass (*Schedonnardus paniculatus*) and *Distichlis stricta*. In the second grass stage buffalograss (*Buchloe dactyloides*) is dominant; other grasses and forbs are of minor importance. As mentioned previously the dominants in the final stage are *Bouteloua gracilis, Stipa comata, Carex* spp., and *Agropyron smithii*.

It is important to note that cyclic replacement change, an intracommunity change, might be confused with directional change, an intercommunity change, which will be discussed in detail later. The upgrade series of the cyclic replacement change is rather conspicuous and might be confused with a successional change, whereas the downgrade series, especially since it often results in bare soil, may be confused with retrogression, i.e., from the more complex to the less complex. In either case, the upgrade or the downgrade cyclic series might be misinterpreted as representing the trend of the community as a whole rather than as the normal internal dynamics of the community.

In summary, replacement change may vary from a simple process to a relatively complex one. The noncyclic change is a simple process on an individual plant basis, while the phasic cycle is a complex one in which several alternative cycles may operate within a given community, forming patches. The replacement change may be operative within the climax or within directional, fluctuational, and intercommunity cyclic changes. In general, the rate varies with the life-span of the component species, especially for the noncyclic replacement change. The rate tends to vary also in the respective series of the cyclic replacement system. The upgrade cyclic series may be confused with a successional change and the downgrade series with a retrogression change, but the cyclic series must be interpreted as the internal dynamics of the community rather than as a directional change of the community itself.

Intercommunity Cycle

The intercommunity cycle is the kind of change whereby one type of community repeatedly changes to another type and then returns to the first one, such as the invasion of a forest by a bog, and then the return of the bog to a forest condition again—reported as occurring in the Upper Kuskokwim River Region, Alaska.[72] If the habitat changes, the vegetation must change. There may be fluctuating climaxes of complementary communities changing in time and space, such as the alternation of steppe and marsh vegetation in a given locality.[205,16,159] Another example is a cyclic development of marshes, above the northern limit of conifers in northern Sweden, beginning with the filling of small lakes with marsh vegetation.[81] Then progressive directional change takes place toward xerophilous heaths rich in lichens, followed by the regeneration of lakes in wind-eroded hollows, and thus the marsh-heath cycle is initiated again.

It is often difficult to determine the nature of changes. For example, an intercommunity cyclic change may have several phases comparable to the upgrade and downgrade sequences as described above for microcommunity cycles. Since a community cyclic-change system would first be apparent in replacements on a microcommunity basis, it might be difficult to differentiate cycles on the community and on the microcommunity units of analysis. Replacement change is undoubtedly operative within the phases of an intercommunity cycle, so the change from one phase to another could be confused readily with directional changes. Thus a change in the upgrade series could be confused with succession, and a change in the downgrade series with retrogression.

Fluctuation Change

Fluctuation change is a random fluctuation about a norm or average. Any given habitat, even a long-persisting one, is never static, irrespective of the time scale used as a reference. The organisms characteristic of the habitat have adaptability to it and its fluctuation changes, and react to such changes in an individual as well as in a collective manner. Regular, cyclic changes of the habitat, such as the usual diurnal daylight and darkness and conditions accompanying the progression of the seasons, are not considered here.

The physical factors of a habitat are constantly fluctuating. Some individual factors may fluctuate independently of the other factors so that there is an infinite complexity of conditions over either a short or a long period of time. These changes of the individual factors and of combinations of factors are fluctuations about the respective means.[196] The variations are characteristic for the respective climatic provinces, localities, and sites; and the climatic elements vary, from year to year, in a random and thus unpredictable manner.

The fluctuations occur over large, local, and small areas. Those over a large area include such categories as climatic region, biotic province, or physiographic province. Generalized information, such as climatic information, is usually available concerning such large areas; the existing meteorological net is applicable to them, but it furnishes only limited climatic information for local areas. The variation in the date of snow disappearance is indicative of local variation.[77] There are also fluctuations between stands and within stands; the meteorological net furnishes no significant climatic information for this scale of area, although there have been limited meteorological studies of certain small areas.

Fluctuations of environmental factors are usually not perceptible with mere observation, especially for a short period of time. Detailed observation and measurement of some factors, such as soil moisture, soil temperature, air temperature, and precipitation are needed for a considerable period to reliably determine the nature of fluctuation changes.

If the fluctuations in the habitat changes are beyond the ecological amplitudes of the existing species, then a fluctuation form of change within the community can be expected. The types and magnitudes of intracommunity fluctuation which result from a complex fluctuation in the habitat are numerous and varied. Fluctuation within the community results from interrelations in both the habitat and the organisms. This becomes manifest in the community in one or a combination of characteristics such as change in kinds of species, dominance, phenology, and growth rate. The seasonal variation in the stage of vegetation development can sometimes be related to the fluctuation of a factor or a complex of factors in the habitat. The date of blooming of 7 species in Utah had a range of 44 days, and this was related to the date of snow disappearance which had a range of 19 days.[77]

Many communities persist for long periods of time with only minor fluctuation in composition. The fluctuations in a steady-state community are rarely of such magnitude that any species is completely eliminated. It is expected that this kind of change would be less apparent in the dominant and characteristic species. Composition change is probably greater in the early stages of succession and less as the steady-state condition is approached. If there is actually a change in species composition in the climax, then such a change is of a relatively temporary duration. Fluctuation may also be manifested in the abundance of a species, and this is probably more common than fluctuation in floristic composition, but even in abundance most species probably exhibit only slight to moderate changes. The fluctuation in abundance of each species tends to be damped and varies around an intermediate position, and as the steady-state is approached the amplitude decreases.

If fluctuation changes are of sufficient amplitude to be significant and of sufficient prominence to be recognized, then it is important to differentiate such changes from other kinds of changes (directional or successional change and cyclic change) so that there will be no confusion as to the kind and significance of the changes.

Directional Change

Directional change is concerned with a noncyclic, reasonably orderly sequence of perceptibly different communities on a given site. A directional change from a less to a more complex community may be considered as a progression, and a change from a more to a less complex community as a retrogression. In some cases the directional change may be deflected to a degree. When

Figure 5-2. The invasion and aggregation of *Poa macrantha* by means of long stolons among the clumps of *Ammophila arenaria* produces an increase in complexity as succession progresses on the sand dune. Oregon. (U.S.D.A. Soil Conservation Service.)

succession occurs in an area where the habitat conditions have been altered by the plants themselves, it is **autogenic;** when altered by agents external to the plants, it is **allogenic.** Directional change must rank as a change of major consequence. This change occurs where the vegetation has not reached a steady-state and the progression culminates in a steady-state, climax community. Directional changes, that is, the stages and processes in succession, have been described in much detail by many writers.[26,47,41,58,198]

Succession is commonly and preferably considered as a progressive development from a simple to a more complex community (Figure 5-2) which usually involves one or more of the

Figure 5-3. Replacement of jack pines (*Pinus banksiana*) in this 70-year-old stand by the balsam fir (*Abies balsamea*) which is capable of growing in the shade of the pines. July, Minnesota. (U. S. Forest Service.)

following: diversity, stability, productivity, self-maintenance, uniformity within and between stands, and soil maturity. This is considered as a positive directional change or a progression.

Each community or ecosystem is in its respective state of flux.[136] Within a nonstable community, development takes place; there are biotic interactions. This gradual development of the vegetation, such as the migration of Sitka spruce (*Picea sitchensis*) westward on Kodiak Island, Alaska, results in a gradual change in the habitat. The habitat is of course also subject to any physical changes which are taking place and which are independent of the biotic influences. The gradual change in habitat is such that the conditions become less suitable for the contemporary species, which are then replaced by species better suited to the new habitat, and thus a new type of community develops (autogenic succession). There is usually a change of species composition, but in some cases the change is in the populations or quantitative relationships of the same species. In either case there is a change in dominants. Within a given region the sequence of dominants tends to be the same. The increase in complexity may be manifest in increased layering of life-forms and greater stature of the dominants. This is related to an increased mass per unit area, or **standing crop,** and usually to greater production of matter per unit area. It is questionable, however, if the final stage in succession always has a greater standing crop than preceding stages. Actual development of the community and modification of the habitat are probably on an intracommunity basis. They consist of directional change sequences on smaller areas within the community. The individual small area of development and change may differ in character from the surrounding parts of the community. These changes on the more minute areas may be completed before the replacement or change of the whole community has run its course (Figure 5-3).

This directional change usually has a starting point and a terminal point, which is the climax vegetation. For example, the **hydrosere** may consist of the submerged, floating, reed-swamp,

Figure 5-4. Primary succession on sand and gravel; first invaders are club-moss (*Selaginella underwoodii*), stonecrop (*Sedum stenopetalum*), *Talinum parviflorum,* and prickly pear (*Opuntia* sp.). Early invading grasses are *Bouteloua gracilis, Poa rupicola,* and *Koeleria cristata.* Virginia Dale, Colorado.

sedge-meadow and woodland stages, and finally the climax forest, while the **xerosere** may consist of the crustose lichen, foliose lichen, moss, herbaceous, and shrub stages, and finally the climax forest.[198] The progression may be regarded as an over-all trend or a general sequence of transformation of plant communities or ecosystems which occupy an area. It is a sequence of replacement of one community by another of a different kind, the result being a procession of communities on a given area, culminating in the

Figure 5-5. Forest fire is an initial cause of secondary succession. August, California. (U.S.D.A. Soil Conservation Service.)

steady-state climax. The actual directional change is gradual and continuous instead of in a series of discrete steps, although subjective vegetation stages can be recognized. The course of the directional change can usually be predicted within a reasonable degree of reliability (Figure 5-4), although the change is not straight or specific, and is subject to a great deal of variation. In some cases successional stages may be skipped or added, or the course of change may be compressed or extended. Use of the term "succession" need not imply the necessity for a large number of stages as in a hydrosere or a xerosere.

An interruption in the sequence of communities may occur. A part or all of the community and habitat may be so changed that an earlier stage of the sequence or a less complex stage occupies the area; this abrupt change may be caused by fire (Figure 5-5), clearing by man, mining, grazing by livestock, wind throw, flooding deposition, landslip, or snowslides. Then a directional sequence starts to run its course again from that stage; this is called secondary succession. The course and rate of directional change within a sere may be rather rapid between some stages (Figures 5-6 and 5-7). In the late summer and fall following cultivation of fields on the Piedmont, North Carolina, crabgrass (*Digitaria sanguinalis*) is usually dominant. During the first year of abandonment, where the fields are not severely eroded, horseweed (*Leptilon canadense*), conspicuous because it is 4 to 6 ft tall, and crabgrass are usually dominant, and ragweed (*Ambrosia elatior*) may share this dominance. During the second year, aster (*Aster pilosus*), approximately 6 ft tall, is usually dominant, and crabgrass and horseweed are still present. During the third year, broomsedge (*Andropogon virginicus*) assumes dominance and maintains the dominance until it is replaced by pines. In due time the climax oaks and hickories occupy the area.[122]

The term "retrogression" is applied by some to a directional change which is essentially the reverse of succession, others include such a change under succession. Retrogression may also be considered partial or gradual destruction of a community, followed by invasion of species characteristic of earlier stages. The causative agent may be climatic, grazing by domestic animals,

Figure 5-6. Change produced by caribou compacting and exposing mineral soil by heavy utilization during the early spring calving season, leads to increased aggregation of *Festuca altaica* in the *Betula glandulosa* community. September, 1957, Black Lake, central Alaska.

Figure 5-7. Change in dense vegetation caused by the pocket gopher (*Thomomys fossor*). August, Grand Mesa National Forest, Colorado. (U. S. Forest Service.)

browsing by wildlife, trampling, reactions of plants, erosion, deposition, repeated flooding, etc. For the direction of change to be maintained as a retrogression, the influence of the causative agent must continue at a certain minimum intensity, such as a uniform rate of deposition, persistence of polygon formation, or mowing. There may be an actual reversal in directional change, such as the change from forest to prairie in Illinois,[88] but Clements[41] denies the existence of a directional change which repeats in reverse order the stages of a succession. A retrogression is not to be confused with a downgrade phase of a cyclic replacement change which is a normal developmental process. Other terms used for retrogression are "degradation" and "destructive change." These terms usually indicate that there are decreases in one or more of the attributes of succession, that is, complexity, diversity, stability, productivity, self-maintenance, uniformity within and between stands, and soil maturity.

Some directional changes may be considered as deflected development.[91] For example, forest, shrubs, and savanna derived from the tropical rain forest and subjected to grazing and recurrent fire, are the result of deflected succession and lead to apparently stable climaxes.[171] The directional change that is usually expected is modified to a significant degree.

The upgrade and downgrade phases of a cyclic replacement change and the intercommunity cyclic change are not to be confused with directional changes. Differentiation must be based on determining that a phasic cycle or an alternating cycle is operative rather than a continuing directional trend. The differentiation between the latter and a phasic cycle is confounded to a degree because a phasic cycle may be operative in succession, such as the alternate establishment and disintegration of the *Danthonia spicata-Cladonia cristatella-C. subtenuis*-moss community until it is finally invaded by *Andropogon virginicus* or *Pinus virginiana*.[195A]

In order to determine that a directional change, such as succession, is taking place, it is necessary either to follow the course of change on a given site, such as permanent sample areas (see Chart 4, p. 104), or to use circumstantial evidence, such as the presence of invading species or of relict species of an earlier stage.

Long-continued studies in the same area, like those of Cooper[54,55] in Glacier Bay, Alaska, are needed.

Summarizing, the stages in the directional change or sequence of communities can be recognized. The changes from the initial establishment of vegetation on an area to the terminal climax community are continuous. However, a given group of species will reach a peak of dominance at a certain stage of the sequence. Then as the dominance of this group decreases, the dominance of another group of species will develop to a maximum. This group is then characteristic as an indicator of its respective stage of the directional change sequence. The change from one stage to the subsequent stage may be especially prominent when there is a change of life-form of the dominant species. There are certain generalizations which can be made concerning the trends in communities when the directional change is a progression. There is usually an increase in productivity per unit of area, in organic mass per unit area because of the presence of the larger life-forms, in complexity and diversity of species and life-forms, and in the relative stability and homogeneity of the populations. The soil and the other aspects of the habitat also undergo progressive development.

Changes in Space

The changes heretofore considered have been within community boundaries. Changes in space resulting in a mosaic of communities, on the other hand, are caused by the distribution of environmental gradients.

As discussed previously, environmental gradients of significant magnitude do occur, they usually persist for a very long period, and there is no known extensive area with a wholly uniform environment. The zone between two communities is considered a reliable indicator of the steepness of the environmental gradient between them. If there is a sharp transition, then the gradient is usually of great magnitude such as that between a sedge-marsh and a dwarf-shrub heath. Bryophytes are especially good indicators of environmental conditions in arctic areas.[62,184] However, if the transition is broad and not well defined, the environmental gradient must be of low magnitude.

The snow-field pattern of vegetation in relation to environmental gradients is common in arctic and alpine areas. The environmental gradients are formed by variations in the depth of snow, duration of snow cover, exposure to wind during winter and summer, length of the growing season, amount and duration of soil moisture, and winter temperatures in the soil, air, and snow cover (see Charts 1 and 2, pp. 18 and 19). The common zonation on lime-poor soil in Norway along the gradients from the exposed top of a ridge to the base of a slope is as follows: *Empetrum hermaphroditum-Louiseleuria procumbens* community, snow cover very thin or not present, exposed to strong winds; *Betula nana* community, snow cover thin, less wind; *Vaccinium myrtillus* community, complete snow cover which melts relatively early; *Deschampsia flexuosa* community, deep snow cover that melts late; and *Salix herbacea* community, very deep snow cover that melts very late or not at all during some years.[86,87]

There may also be spatial changes within a community. These changes are likewise caused by significant environmental gradients. The gradients or microgradients within the community are in some cases as great or greater in magnitude than the gradient between two communities. The differences in the *Calluna*, *Cladonia*, bare soil, and *Arctostaphylos* phases of the dwarf Callunetum community described by Watt[197] may indeed be greater than the difference between this community and the adjacent community. The magnitude of microgradients within each community is probably distinctive for the respective community.

If the gradients remain unchanged for long periods of time, the mosaic of communities remains unchanged and each community thereon is in the steady-state. However, if the environment of one sector or of all the gradient is changing rather rapidly, then there will be directional change taking place in one or more communities on such areas, so that the mosaic is changing.

During a long period of time the actual spatial position of the environmental gradients may change very slowly. This may be due to slow-acting geological processes, among which are normal geologic erosion, block uplift, glacial retreat, and climatic change. Such changes are at so slow a rate, that usually no significant alteration occurs during the period of field study conducted by one investigator. The same pattern of communities usually persists, even though the spatial disposition of each changes.

Rate of Change

The rate of any type of change is important. The analysis of changes within a community and between communities is facilitated by determining the rate of each, preferably in absolute, but at least in relative, terms.

An indication of the rate of development or succession of a lichen community may be found in the fact that lichens of the family Umbelicariaceae require several hundred years to attain full growth,[62] so these lichens are, of course, absent where solifluction occurs. A good example of a study showing the rate of succession following the retreat of glaciers is that of Cooper, at Glacier Bay, Alaska.[54,55] The duration of stages in secondary succession on old fields and on forest lands has also been given by several writers.[41,46,122]

The permanence of many communities in arctic and alpine areas indicates that changes in the habitat are not significant or that the species present in rapidly changing habitats such as solifluction areas, are adapted to them either by special structural features or by wide ranges in ecological amplitude. The duration and stability in Scandinavia of arctic and alpine plant communities not influenced by man, even of the half-open grass-heath communities such as those of *Kobresia myosuroides* and *Festuca ovina*, have been stressed.[151] The habitats and vegetation of polygons on Akpatok Island have probably changed very little in 1000 to 2000 years.[165]

The numerous arctic and alpine species which survived glaciation in refuges, as indicated by biogeographic evidence, have had a long time in which to form communities of great stability. Evidence for the great age of the arctic and alpine flora in Scandinavia is seen particularly in the relatively large number of endemic species and the presence of a large west arctic element comprising many species of herbs, lichens, and mosses. This element is present also in Iceland and Greenland as well as being widely distributed in North America.[61]

CLIMAX

It has been mentioned that the culmination of a directional change is a steady-state, climax community in which no further directional change takes place under the prevailing environmental conditions. This is the terminus of habitat and vegetation development. The climax will be discussed because the ability to determine whether a community is a successional or a climactic one is important.

The criteria of a climax community serve primarily to differentiate it from a successional community. The differentiation is both subjective and relative, so that the criteria cannot be highly specific. Each criterion is independent, to a degree, of the other criteria. Furthermore, each may have enough exceptions so that it cannot be employed to the exclusion of the others. The criteria must be used with a degree of subjectivity dependent upon the skill and judgment of the investigator.

The climax community is in the steady-state with respect to productivity, structure, and population, with the dynamic balance of its populations dependent upon its respective site. The community has a maximum diversity, relative stability, and homogeneity of the species populations within and between the stands of a given climax type. Each stand is self-maintaining and relatively permanent. The stand persists for a long time with little or no change (Figures 5-8 and 5-8A). Any change consists of an interplay of populations, i.e., fluctuation change, even though replacement on a microcommunity basis may be a phasic cycle. There is neither a beginning nor an end of such fluctuation change in time. The given climax type is characterized by its physiognomy or homogeneity in appearance within and between stands. However, a maximum of spatial stratification can be expected, and this balanced structure of several growth-forms and maximum diversity of species provides a system which apparently permits fullest use of the environment and maximum production on a sustained basis.

The composition and population of the climax are determined by all factors of the mature ecosystem, not by any one factor. These factors are the properties of each species, biotic interrelations, floristic and faunistic availability, chances of dispersion, interaction, soils, climate, and possibly special factors such as fire, wind, snow, and salt spray.

Climax vegetation may be considered, according to Whittaker,[205] as a pattern of populations corresponding to the pattern of environmental gradients. The relationships among the populations change with alterations in these gradients. The vegetation pattern is more or less diverse in accordance with the diversity of the environmental complex, and the composition of the climax type is meaningful only in relation to its particular spatial position on the environmental gradient. There is convergence or succession to similar structural-functional population patterns in similar environments, yet this is partly independent of the original environmental conditions and the course of development. There is a homogeneity between stands on similar sites, and any varia-

Figure 5-8. A vigorous clump of *Bouteloua gracilis*. August, San Antonio, Texas. (U.S.D.A. Soil Conservation Service.)

tions usually indicate the degree of stabilization. Thus there is a mosaic of climax types which corresponds to the mosaic of habitats or environmental gradients.[189]

An example of a mosaic of climax types is the dwarf shrub-heath in Sikilsdalen, Norway, which was divided into two alliances differing in relative species composition and abundance chiefly in response to the amount and duration of snow cover in the habitat.[151] The more xeric of the alliances has 7 associations, of which one, the Empetreto-Betuletum nanae, is an example of a pattern in relation to environmental gradients. This association is separated into 4 sociations, chiefly on the basis of differences in the proportion of several species of lichens; *Betula nana,* the chief vascular dominant, is found in about equal abundance in each sociation. The *Betula nana-Alectoria ochroleuca* sociation occurs in sites that have the least snow cover, dry most rapidly in the spring, and are so exposed to the wind that pieces of the lichen mass are torn loose. It is characterized by high frequency and cover of the lichen, *Alectoria ochroleuca.* There are also other wind-resistant lichens. The second community, the *Betula nana-Empetrum herma-phroditum-Cetraria nivalis* sociation, often alternating with the

Figure 5-8A. Roots of blue gramagrass are very numerous here, some extending to a depth of 4 ft. This short-grass is well adapted to drought and grazing, and is a component of a number of climax communities. Willcox, Arizona. (U.S.D.A. Soil Conservation Service.)

Figure 5-9. A climax stand of *Cladonia alpestris*, with intermixed dwarf shrubs and herbs. Excellent winter range for caribou or reindeer, widespread in Subarctic in North America and Scandinavia. July, 1957, near Paxson, Alaska.

first, is found in depressions in rough terrain and in more sheltered sites, so that it has more snow cover and is less exposed to the wind. The third, the *Betula nana-Cladonia alpestris* sociation (Figure 5-9), is characterized particularly by the vigor and height of *C. alpestris*. It occurs in still better-protected sites, the snow cover is deeper and lasts longer, and it is less exposed to the wind. The site is weakly mesic in contrast to the previous xeric ones, and there are indications in the soil profile of weak solifluction. The fourth community, the *Betula nana-Cladonia rangiferina-C. silvatica* sociation—characterized by these two lichens, more moss, and *Salix glauca*—tolerates still deeper and longer-enduring snow cover, the substratum is more moist, and the soil profile shows the effects of solifluction. This community often occurs on solifluction terraces. The gradients in environmental factors from the first to the fourth community are: increasing depth and duration of snow cover associated with less exposure to wind, probably a later inception of growth in the spring, increasing soil moisture, and increasing likelihood of solifluction.

The changes which are expected within the steady-state are replacement change and fluctuation change. The upgrade and downgrade phases of a cyclic replacement change could be prominent, and be misleading in determining that the steady-state exists. It has already been noted that fluctuation changes are usually not perceptible by simple observation, especially over a short period of time.

In summary, the criteria to differentiate a climax community from a successional community are subjective and relative. The climax community is in the steady-state with respect to productivity, structure, and population (Figure 5-10). There is a diversity, stability, and homogeneity of the species populations within and between stands of the same climax community. Each stand is self-maintaining and long-persisting. Replacement and fluctuation changes are operative on a continuing basis within the climax, while all environmental factors determine its composition and population so that there is a mosaic of climax types corresponding to the mosaic of habitats.

Conclusions

One of the more important and difficult tasks of the ecologist is to determine the dynamics within and between communities and especially the successional or climax status of each community. Five kinds of significant change are: replacement, intercommunity cycle, directional and fluctuation changes in the same place, and change in space. Succession is one type of change —a very important kind. The analysis of changes provides a

Figure 5-10. A climax forest of virgin hemlock (*Tsuga canadensis*), with aggregations of the broadleaf evergreen, *Rhododendron maximum*, in the shrub layer. May, Clarion County, Pennsylvania. (U. S. Forest Service.)

useful means to assign the proper status to successional and climax communities.

Environmental gradients are present in all areas. The patterns of long-enduring environmental gradients occur with respect to many factors such as the presence, areal extent, depth, and duration of snow-cover, exposure to wind and to insolation, soil moisture, drainage, nature of substratum, occurrence and degree of soil movement, freezing action, and presence of salt. The presence and nature of gradients can be determined readily in some places, with difficulty in others. The patterns of different communities can be recognized in relation to the environmental gradients, and are formed especially by populations of the more sensitive species. In order to have only one type of community over a very large area it would be necessary to have a nongradient environment over the entire area, which cannot be attained since geomorphic processes are operating continuously, although often very slowly. Consequently the types of gradients will usually remain essentially the same, for example the shift of snow patches, or the increase in their size. It is conceivable that an environmental condition at one or the other end of the gradient might be eliminated. However, if the gradients present at the time have reached the steady-state, then for a significant period the pattern of gradients and their associated climax communities will remain essentially the same, even though the actual disposition may change to some indeterminate degree.

The communities on the long-enduring gradients have a high degree of stability and organization. The principal species in each kind are well adjusted in their reactions to one another, such as shading and accumulation of organic matter. Similar communities and similar patterns of communities are present in separated areas in which environmental conditions are similar. So long as environmental conditions remain substantially the same, the communities appear to undergo fluctuations about a mean, rather than directional change. These long-enduring communities have the attributes of climax communities and fit well into a climax mosaic pattern along environmental gradients.

The presence of phasic cycles may be the cause, or one of the causes, of questioning the applicability of a climax status to some climax areas, especially if the investigator does not realize he is dealing with a phasic cycle. The apparent lack of stability between individual phases may contribute to this opinion, especially when a downgrade change is taking place and is prominent. However, if the phasic cycle is analyzed as a whole in relation to surrounding vegetation, the community will be found to fulfill the criteria of the climax since the phasic cycle is operative within the climax framework. If the upgrade phases, inclusive of the most complex phase, are predominant in the area and give the community its aspect, then the vegetation might be interpreted as a successional stage. If, on the other hand, the downgrade phases are predominant, the vegetation might be interpreted as a retrogression stage. Either error is serious because it may lead to the conclusion that a climax status is not applicable.

The change from one cyclic phase to another phase is certainly directional in detail, whether it is upgrade or downgrade, for there is a change in the habitat, kinds of species, abundance, and life-forms. However, considered as repetitive cycles, there is no directional change. The cycle as a whole is within the limits of the criteria of the steady-state, but a single phase may not meet such criteria. A long-term study of the phasic cycle will reveal that as a whole any over-all changes will take on the qualities of a fluctuation change instead of the radical alterations which are so prominent between two succeeding phases. The pattern of microcommunities and populations is related to the pattern of mesogradients and of microgradients of the habitat. It is just as valid to consider phasic cycle changes and stages as inherent processes and parts of the climax steady-state as it is to consider the changes and stages following the death of an occasional tree in the forest or the death of clumps of blue gramagrass (*Bouteloua gracilis*) in a grassland climax as such.

In the application of the climax concept, the alternation of communities, or an intercommunity cyclic change, may present more difficulty than microcommunity alternation or cyclic change because of the apparent lack of stability of each phasic community and of the cycle as a whole. The downgrade phase, especially, is often difficult to interpret correctly, but when such a cycle is analyzed as a whole, the changes satisfy the climax criteria.

The change from community to community in place, even though phasic, is easily confused with a directional change which would be successional if the change were upgrade, and retrogressional if the change were downgrade. This change may proceed horizontally in lieu of being exclusively in place. The confusion with succession and retrogression arises readily because of the alterations in habitat conditions. The change from one community phase of the cycle to the next one probably operates similarly to a replacement. In fact, during part of the community-to-community change it may be very difficult to differentiate it from a replacement phasic cycle. Fluctuations within the community cyclic change are expected, and therefore a degree of variation will occur in the habitat, species, and populations. But when the cycle is analyzed as a whole, it will be found that the changes are within circumscribed limits which satisfy the criteria of a climax, in spite of the conspicuous alterations between phases.

At first it seems that directional changes offer no difficulty in assigning a succession or retrogression, rather than a climax, status to a community; generally, if a directional change is taking place, the community under consideration does not satisfy the criteria of a climax. However, the rate of change from a near-terminal stage to the climax is usually very slow, much slower than between the earlier stages of a successional series; in fact the changes may not be perceptible during the study-span of one person. Furthermore, the near-terminal stage may have many of the attributes of a climax.

Fluctuations of small magnitude usually cause no difficulty, but fluctuations of relatively great magnitude can easily cause trouble in the applicability of the climax concept. For a particular type of climax community, a certain magnitude of fluctuation change is expected and is within the framework of the steady-state. A fluctuation change of relatively great magnitude in a community may be confused with a phasic cycle replacement change which is not characteristic of the particular community, and intensive study over a long period of time may be required to differentiate between them. Fluctuation change does not occur exclusively in the climax, but occurs also in successional stages. The magnitude of fluctuation is probably greater in the seral stages than in the near-terminal and climax, but the magnitude cannot be used as a criterion to differentiate a succession stage and a climax.

An analysis of the environmental gradients and of each type of change within and between communities provides a reliable means of determining the successional or climax status. The steady-state communities making up mosaic patterns corresponding to the patterns of long-enduring environmental gradients are considered as climax. Such changes as do occur in these communities are regarded as being within the framework of the climax.

GENERAL REFERENCES

Churchill, E. D. and Hanson, H. C., "The Concept of Climax in Arctic and Alpine Vegetation," *Botan. Rev.,* **24,** 127–191 (1958).

Clements, F. E., "Plant Succession," *Carnegie Inst. Washington Publ.,* No. 242 (1916).

Conard, H. S., "The Background of Plant Ecology" (trans. from the German of Kerner, A., 1863, "The Plant Life of the Danube Basin"), Iowa State College Press, Ames, 1951.

Cowles, H. C., "The Causes of Vegetative Cycles," *Botan. Gaz.,* **51,** 161–183 (1911).

Tansley, A. G., "The Use and Abuse of Vegetation Concepts and Terms," *Ecology,* **16,** 284–307 (1935).

Watt, A. S., "Pattern and Process in the Plant Community," *Jour. Ecol.,* **35,** 1–22 (1947).

Whittaker, R. H., "A Consideration of the Climax Theory: The Climax as a Population and Pattern," *Ecol. Monogr.,* **23,** 41–78 (1953).

PART FOUR

Classification of Communities

BASES AND UNITS

BASES OF CLASSIFICATION

An extensive area of vegetation varies from one part to another because of differences in topography such as north and south slopes, soil conditions, or stages of succession. A large area presents too much complexity in vegetation and environmental conditions to study as a whole, so it must be separated into subdivisions that are usually recognized by dissimilarities in physiognomy, species composition, or often in topography. Each basic unit is a stand, or individual plant community—an aggregation of species with considerable uniformity in structure and composition, and occupying an area of highly uniform environment.[144] Each stand has its own individuality, and is marked by the possession of certain biotypes, and often ecotypes also, that are not found in other, similar stands;[140,141] however, a number of biotypes or ecotypes may be present in common in several stands.

Delimitation of a stand is not difficult when it has sharp boundaries (Figures 1-4 and 1-20), which may be caused by abrupt changes or steep gradients in the substratum, by reactions of plants to shading, or by fire, grazing, or cultivation. Delimitation is more difficult when the gradients are gradual, and abrupt changes in the vegetation do not appear. However, as the gradient changes, due, for example, to a decrease in soil moisture, some species become less numerous and others become more so, creating an effect comparable to the gradual changing of color in the spectrum, in which measured portions have been delimited as blue, yellow, red, etc.[200] Similarly, the vegetation on a gradient (a **cline**) can be quantitatively segregated into units on the basis of measurements of numerical abundance, cover, and frequency, especially of the constant and characteristic species (see p. 125).[200] For example, in the lower part of a cline *Agropyron smithii* and *Stipa viridula* may each average 25 per cent or more in foliage cover and 100 per cent in frequency, and in the same part *Bouteloua gracilis* and *Stipa comata* may each rate less than 10 per cent in cover and 40 per cent in frequency. As one ascends the slope the former pair gradually decreases in cover and frequency, while the latter increases, until the figures may be reversed, thus forming a different stand. The demarcation of the two stands may be placed where the cover of the second pair exceeds that of the first, and where the frequency of the second pair rises above 80 per cent while that of the other pair falls below this percentage. The portion of the cline where the data for all four species are closely similar may be considered as another stand, or a transitional zone.

Transition zones, as a rule, are readily recognized by the presence in them of species from each of the adjacent stands, and often by changes in structure and greater heterogeneity. It is usually advisable to delay analysis of these zones until a frame of reference of well-marked stands has become available. It is also good procedure to make a reconnaissance study of an extensive area of vegetation first before beginning intensive analysis of the constituent stands, so that a general idea of the different kinds of stands or types of vegetation may be gained.

Description of a stand, as of other entities, should be based upon an analysis which reveals as many of the intrinsic qualities as possible. It appears obvious that vegetation should be characterized by its own properties and not by extrinsic data, but the illogical procedure of using the habitat, or the stage of ecologic succession, as part of the characterization of a community is a custom of long standing.[179] The environment is a controlling influence, not a property, of vegetation and the successional status is often hypothetical, though important. The most commonly used intrinsic qualities are both analytic and synthetic (see Chapters 3 and 4), and include kinds of species, life-form, population density, cover, frequency, stratification, periodicity, dominance, vitality, and physiognomy. However, many descriptions of vegetation are inadequate because only two or three of these are considered, while a good description, to be complete, must include most of the qualitative and quantitative properties, with analytic tables as well as good verbal description. Each feature of the community is important, especially in relation to the environment, and a single approach, such as emphasis on dominance, as among some American ecologists, or on characteristic and differential species, as among some phytosociologists, is not adequate. According to Poore, "The more accurate and detailed the information the more valuable the description, which includes as a matter of course the examination of the soil profile and accurate notes on certain features of the habitat. Description by physiognomy and dominance alone, on the other hand, may cause one to ignore the detail for wider aspects, and even to consider that a description of the dominant and striking species is the same thing as a description of the synecology of the community." [166,p.45]

Usually the most important criterion in classification is similarity, so stands possessing a number of characteristics in common, particularly in species composition and structure, and occupying similar habitats, are placed in one community-type. The recurrence of similar stands in similar habitats has been demonstrated by many investigators.[151,25,191,144,72,103] The relation of stand to habitat is so close (Figure 1-27) that even in the Arctic it has been found possible to predict the vegetation type with a fair degree of reliability when the soil profile and general geographic location are known.[191] Although it is true that the complexity of floristic and environmental conditions is so great that the exact combination and sequence of events are seldom if ever repeated,[74] yet, as in any kind of classification, exact duplication or likeness is not essential for grouping stands into abstract categories. The degree of similarity needed for placing stands in the same community-type or association requires careful judgment; but, as in evaluations of many biological phenomena such as stages in mitosis, different investigators have been found to agree closely in their decisions. In placing stands in community-types, an increase in objectivity is secured by employing quantitative criteria such as the coefficient-of-similarity.[25,62,127,103] While similarity is the chief criterion in classifying stands, a certain degree of relationship, or affinity, is also present because of the common evolutionary origin of individuals of a species and because of interactions such as pollination, and obviously the greater the number of species in common, the greater will be the affinity.

In some places, very small units, such as a square meter or only a few square centimeters, of various kinds of vegetation occur repeatedly. These variations in species composition are caused by changes in the environment, particularly in the substratum. For example, the top of a mound in a bog or marsh may have a very different plant cover from that in the depressions, and the north and south sides of a single mound may vary greatly, especially in the Arctic and Subarctic. Such small units are microstands, each kind with its inherent characteristics and specific habitat conditions. The aggregate of such microstands in an area may be considered as a **community-complex** when there is some order or pattern in distribution as on the borders of lakes or ponds, on sand dunes, around ant-hills, and on snow-bed areas in alpine regions. When the microstands are intermixed without any apparent pattern, as commonly occurs in marshes and bogs, the conglomeration may be considered as a **community-mosaic**.[127] The vegetation on mounds in the tundra may consist largely of wind-resistant lichens and low shrubs, while in the depressions mosses, other kinds of lichens, and taller shrubs grow. It is often desirable to treat the entire mosaic or complex as a unit, but each of the various kinds of microstands composing it must be analyzed to secure a full understanding of the vegetation. Similar microstands in a mosaic or complex may be grouped into a microcommunity-type; thus mosaics or complexes may be considered to consist of several kinds of microcommunity-types, and, obviously, they may also be classified into higher categories on the basis of similarity.

For each stand and community-type, in addition to an analysis of the intrinsic characteristics, a description is needed of the habitat, the position on environmental gradients, and, whenever possible, the successional status. A description of the habitat should include at least a general statement about temperature and precipitation, topography, nature of the substratum including a profile description, and an appraisal of limiting or critical factors. The successional status of various stands ranges from an early stage in primary or secondary succession to the climax. Consequently, the dynamic or syngenetic position of every community needs to be considered, especially the development or growth from a young to a mature stand, succession or the replacement of one stand by another, and the evolution or changes in the community by means of the genic modification of constituent species that occurs, as well as the other changes discussed in Chapter 5. Since mutations apparently do not, as a rule, persist in natural vegetation, it can be expected that a community will be long-enduring provided that the environment does not change greatly, but alteration of the environment or in the kinds and numbers of species in the stand may give opportunity for mutations to become established. Studies in dynamics require the preservation of samples of natural communities, not only for the maintenance of gene pools, but also because the complex interrelationships of the organisms in each have required a long period of inter-coordinated ecologic evolution which cannot be duplicated by man.

CRITERIA OF CLASSIFICATION (SYNSYSTEMATICS)

Many kinds of plant communities, differing in magnitude and complexity, may be found in any country, and almost instinctively one tends to place them in groups, such as forest, grassland, or weedy wasteland. The human mind apparently demands orderliness, so classification is more than a convenience,[200] it is an

LAND CAPABILITY CLASSES			
SUITABLE FOR CULTIVATION		NO CULTIVATION - PASTURE, HAY, WOODLAND AND WILDLIFE	
I	REQUIRES GOOD SOIL MANAGEMENT PRACTICES ONLY	V	NO RESTRICTIONS IN USE
II	MODERATE CONSERVATION PRACTICES NECESSARY	VI	MODERATE RESTRICTIONS IN USE
III	INTENSIVE CONSERVATION PRACTICES NECESSARY	VII	SEVERE RESTRICTIONS IN USE
IV	PERENNIAL VEGETATION - INFREQUENT CULTIVATION	VIII	BEST SUITED FOR WILDLIFE AND RECREATION

Figure 6-1. A practical kind of classification based chiefly on susceptibility of the soil to erosion, widely used by the Soil Conservation Service in determining the capability of land for various uses. (U.S.D.A. Soil Conservation Service.)

essential aid in organizing facts and in promoting clear thinking. There are many kinds of data arrangement, and even a classification of classifications was presented as long ago as 1813 by de Candolle,[109] who recognized the following types:

   (1) Empirical, such as alphabetical, not based on the intrinsic nature of the objects
   (2) Rational, based on the nature of the objects
       (a) Practical, concerned with values to man (Figure 6-1)
       (b) Artificial, using characters that facilitate arrangement and identification
       (c) Natural, employing affinities between organisms

There are many approaches to the rational classification of vegetation units, and since these units themselves are more or less arbitrarily delimited, the classifications are likewise arbitrary.[207,93] Various characteristics have been employed as the chief criteria, the choice depending largely upon the purpose and viewpoint of the classifier, widely used ones being species composition, physiognomy and life-form, and the successional status. In empirical classification one of the most widely used criteria, partly because of its convenience, is the nature of the habitat. The choice of criteria is influenced greatly by the geographic extent of the vegetation, by one's knowledge of the plants, and the time and facilities that are available for field work. Reconnaissance of a 100-sq-mile area, especially in a little-known region, requires the use of different criteria from those employed in the analysis and mapping of types on only a few square miles or less.

When extensive areas are being investigated, differentiation, as a rule, is first made of large physiognomic units such as coniferous forest, deciduous forest, shrubland, and grassland (Figures 1-1 and 2-6). Each of these units may then be subdivided on the basis of life-form, dominance, successional status, or habitat. Some workers, as Rübel, Brockman-Jerosch, and Däniker, have stated that it is impossible to synthesize large units from the analysis and description of small communities,[11] but others, including Braun-Blanquet[25,26] and Tüxen,[195] maintain the opposite viewpoint, and have produced systems of vegetation by this inductive method. In a limited area such as a few square miles, small units, recognized chiefly on the basis of homogeneity in species composition, may well serve as the starting point.

Five major criteria, listed below, have been widely used in the classification of plant communities and will be discussed and examples of their use given.

(1) Floristic or species composition
(2) Ecological relations or habitat
(3) Successional status
(4) Physiognomy
(5) Geographical characteristics

The floristic criterion is the most basic one in segregating units of vegetation because it deals more intensively and adequately with the inherent nature of each unit, including data on the other criteria. It is often more convenient to use one of the others, but a complete, scientific classification requires consideration of species composition, in addition to the other analytic and synthetic characteristics, of the various kinds of stands occurring in each group distinguished by any of the last four major criteria listed above. In America classification based on the first criterion is less common because of the lack of sufficient plant sociological analysis, the use of one of the others being more prevalent than in Europe. Progress in America in the classification of vegetation on the basis of inherent characters requires more detailed analyses of the communities making up the large heterogeneous units.

Floristic or Species Composition

Classification on the basis of floristic characteristics or species composition is based strictly on intrinsic properties of the community, as shown especially in plant sociological tables (see Tables 3-1 and 4-1). Some stands have more characteristic species in common than others, so they are placed in one community-type, and similar community-types are placed in one group. Such grouping of similar entities is essential for more complete comprehension and orderly presentation of isolated data developed by analytic methods.

In sociological analysis a number of inherent qualities are used, and since in classification the number of criteria is limited, emphasis is placed upon those qualities that are considered the most significant. Ecological characterization of the units is also included. In some countries, chiefly Norway and Sweden, the dominant species (those with greatest numerical abundance or cover and frequency) and constant species are employed for arranging stands into sociations and associations, and characteristic species (see p. 127) have been used for placing associations into higher categories: alliance, order, and class.[151,11] In many other countries, particularly in central and western Europe, following Braun-Blanquet, the most widely employed are characteristic species (those in one of the three highest classes of fidelity). The **differentiating species,** which distinguish between groups by their absence or lesser occurrence in one group than in others, and dominants (see p. 128) are also important here, especially in the segregation of minor categories.

These attributes—kinds of species, abundance, frequency, dominance, and fidelity—have been used to make a hierarchical system of classification, including the association with its sub-divisions and variants to alliance, order, and class. Associations belonging to one alliance are represented by stands within a certain area, or in corresponding habitats in other areas. For example, in a limited area in the mountain-front zone in northern Colorado the major kinds of grassland have been classified according to the limited data now available,[103] as follows:

(1) *Andropogon scoparius-A. gerardi-Stipa comata* alliance

   (a) *Andropogon scoparius* association
   (b) *Stipa comata-Bouteloua gracilis-B. curtipendula* association
   (c) *Bouteloua gracilis-Artemisia glauca* association

(2) *Agropyron smithii-Bromus tectorum* alliance

   (d) *Agropyron smithii-Bouteloua gracilis-Bromus tectorum* association

The habitats of the stands in the first alliance were marked by more or less erosion, shallow to moderately shallow soils, and usually much gravel and rock. The habitats of the other alliance were distinguished by deposition, and deep and compact soils containing very little gravel and rock in the upper 6 in. In successional status all appeared to be in the climax or near-climax stage under the prevailing conditions.

Conard,[48] classified the most important associations in Iowa into about eight orders, the first one with two alliances and six associations, as follows:

(1) Reed order, *Phragmitetalia*

    (*a*) Reed alliance, *Phragmition,* with the following associations:

        Reed, *Phragmitetum communis iowenses*
        Bulrush, *Scirpetum validi*
        Cattail, *Typhetum*
        Reed canarygrass, *Phalaridetum arundinaceae*
        Sloughgrass, *Spartinetum pectinatae*

    (*b*) Sedge alliance, *Magnocaricion,* with one association:
        Sedge, *Caricetum strictae*

Conard points out that the classification he used permitted (1) the arrangement of communities in a logical sequence from aquatic habitats to grassland and woodland, (2) the showing of similarities between communities on the basis of floristic composition, and (3) comparison with communities in other parts of the world.

The increasing emphasis on dominant and constant species by those using the Braun-Blanquet procedures indicates an important convergence of central and northern European methods, as apparently there are no important or basic differences between them.[11] These procedures have been thoroughly tested recently in Britain and their advantages pointed out,[166] and they deserve far more attention in America than they have received so far.[103,101,48]

The number of communities within a region distinguished by these sociological attributes may be very large. For example, the nitrophilous weed communities in the Eurosiberian Region of Europe were classified and characterized into 132 associations, 26 alliances, 10 orders, and 6 classes,[195] a work entailing very many analyses of stands, numerous sociological tables, and descriptions by many workers. These associations are eminently suitable for differentiating the smallest communities in various habitats, and in systematic classification they are indispensable.[127]

However, the small units are less suitable for describing the vegetation of an extensive territory because of the difficulty of gaining an over-all viewpoint. In order to solve this problem, large units, called **principal-associations** (Hauptassoziationen), each usually occupying an extensive area, have been proposed by Knapp[127]—for example, the oak-hornbeam principal-association extending from western to eastern Europe. The characterization and delimitation of these large units are based on sociological analyses and descriptions of almost innumerable stands, such as those of the characteristic species *Carpinus betulus, Prunus avium,* and *Potentilla sterilis* in the oak-hornbeam forest, in which the chief attribute for delimitation is high constancy. Subdivisions, called **regional-associations** (Gebiets-assoziationen), are distinguished by differential species, floral history, and some features of the habitat. Examples in the United States of Knapp's principal-association appear to be the oak-hickory forests of the central and eastern parts of the country and the *Bouteloua-Buchloe* grasslands of the Great Plains.

Ecological Relations or Habitat

Classification on the basis of ecological relations (synecology) has been widely used. This is a causal approach that requires an analysis of the environment and the segregation of habitat types, which involves difficult problems, for the habitat factors governing the occurrence of species and communities are not readily measured and interpreted. Usually observations and interpretations of relationships have been limited to the major conditions such as geographic location, physiography (altitude, slope, soil), and general climatic influences, without including detailed quantitative data. However, large environmental complexes can be used advantageously in distinguishing the main kinds of vegetation (Figure 1-4), later dividing them into their components, as was done in a study in the mountains of Scotland[167] in which most of the communities fit into a framework of the following five factor complexes:

(1) Altitudinal zonation: forest, up to about 2100 feet; above it, subalpine, potential birch woodland; low alpine; very little middle alpine
(2) Oceanicity: change from oceanic climate near the coasts to continental climate in the interior, including higher

Figure 6-2. Zonation around a pond near Palmer, Alaska. (1) Yellow water-lily (*Nuphar polysepalum*) in the deeper water; (2) buckbean (*Menyanthes trifoliata*) and *Potentilla palustris* in shallow water; (3) *Potentilla palustris, Calamagrostis* sp., and *Sphagnum* on wet substratum; (4) hummocky substratum with species as in (3) and willows, alder, and glandular birch; and (5) zone of dead birch trees, surrounded by the birch-white spruce forest. June.

summer maxima temperatures, lower winter minima, more rapid transitions in spring and in autumn, longer growing period, and less prevalence of high winds

(3) Snow cover: duration and depth

(4) Chemical composition of the soil, especially bases

(5) Soil moisture

In the detailed analysis of vegetation the environmental approach has not been very successful. It is more satisfactory and logical first to distinguish and describe stands by their own intrinsic qualities, particularly species composition and relative abundance, and then to try to determine the causative influences. The species composition can be observed and measured directly, but the causes may be difficult to unravel and must often be inferred from the occurrence of certain plants, particularly those

Figure 6-3. This grassland under moderate grazing is approaching through succession the terminal grassland stage. Western yellow pine (*Pinus ponderosa*) and Douglas fir (*Pseudotsuga taxifolia*) are shown in the background. July, Pikes Peak Region, Colorado. (U. S. Forest Service.)

with narrow ecological amplitude, and from observations (or rather crude measurements) of habitat conditions. Segregation of communities on the basis of their location on gradients involves difficulties, for usually there are gradients in a number of factors, such as soil moisture, soil salts, pH, and temperature, each influencing the vegetation simultaneously (Figure 6-2). If the controlling influences in the gradients are known and can be measured, and if equilibrium between vegetation and the environmental complex exists, then it would appear possible to establish the composition of the community as a function of the position on the ecological gradient. However, "the ecological gradients of importance to vegetation are unknown at the beginning of an investigation of the vegetation of an area and cannot be guessed beforehand," [62,p.79] so the ordination of communities according to ecological gradients[93] is very difficult. There appears to be general agreement that the basis for securing understanding of nature must be the study of directly observable characters, and not hypothetical inferences about the relations between vegetation and the environment.[62]

Successional Status

Classification of units on the basis of succession (syndynamics) has been widely used in the United States and in other countries where emphasis on plant physiology and plant processes is strong, and also where natural vegetation occurs following the destruction of the original plant cover or where it was greatly disturbed by man or animals. The most exhaustive classification based on this criterion, **vegetation dynamics,** is by Clements in his book "Plant Succession."[41] An example illustrating the use of stages in secondary succession in classifying the vegetation types is taken from a study on abandoned crop land in the Pike's Peak region in Colorado (Figure 6-3).[116]

(1) Initial stage: annual forbs and grasses
(2) Perennial forb stage: perennial weedy forbs, grasses, and a few shrubs, persists for 3 to 5 years after cessation of cultivation
(3) Mixed grass and weed stage
    (a) *Stipa-Agropyron* phase, duration about 10 years
    (b) *Stipa-Bouteloua phase,* develops within 15 to 25 years after abandonment
(4) Subclimax bunchgrass stage: *Muhlenbergia montana* and *Festuca arizonica* as dominants
(5) Climax: *Pinus ponderosa* and *Pseudotsuga taxifolia* as dominants

In each of these stages several kinds of communities may be present; for example, in the first stage nearly pure stands of *Setaria viridis, Chenopodium album,* and *Helianthus annuus* are found, as well as mixtures of these and other species. It is important to analyze and describe the communities in each stage, but too often this has not been done. Such analysis would undoubtedly reveal many community-soil relationships and differences in the course of succession in relation to site conditions.

The successional approach has limited usefulness in areas

where the communities have considerable stability,[62] and difficulties are often encountered in deciding if succession is actually taking place. Furthermore, classification by successional status in many instances cannot avoid a considerable degree of assumption. Consequently, this criterion is not as sound as others. As has been stated before, the analysis and classification of stands do not require precise determination of the successional position, for, without minimizing the importance of this position, the kinds and rates of change that are occurring in a community can best be treated in the description following the sociological analysis. It is not desirable to inject successional stages into a plant sociological classification, or, in other words, to mix the criteria of successional status and floristic composition.[38]

Physiognomy

Physiognomy is dependent upon a number of qualitative and quantitative characteristics, especially life-form, as well as upon structure and dominance. This basis of classification is very useful in distinguishing and delimiting major types of communities such as coniferous forest and deciduous forest, or shortgrass and tallgrass communities. The use of physiognomy is important in the preliminary reconnaissance of an area, to ascertain the major types of vegetation, for mapping purposes, and as a start for subdividing the major types into the constituent communities. For example, in the mountain-front region of northern Colorado the vegetation consists of zones and mosaics of stands of various kinds, mostly grassland and shrub, chiefly the mixed mid- and shortgrass type (*Stipa comata-Bouteloua gracilis-B. curtipendula*), the medium tall grassland (*Andropogon scoparius*), the mixed perennial-annual grassland (*Agropyron smithii-Bouteloua gracilis-Bromus tectorum*), and shrub types (*Cercocarpus montanus, Rhus trilobata, Symphoricarpos* sp., and *Physocarpus monogynus*).[101]

Classification based chiefly or solely on physiognomy is most valuable in the first studies in a region where little is known about the vegetation, and in aerial surveys, but even in such studies whenever it is possible, the various communities constituting each physiognomic group should be characterized analytically and synthetically. As an example of this criterion, the system proposed by Dansereau[63] includes six series of characters, as follows:

(1) Life-form: trees, shrubs, herbs, bryoids, epiphytes, and lianas
(2) Size: tall, medium, and low
(3) Function: deciduous, semideciduous, evergreen, evergreen-succulent, and evergreen-leafless
(4) Shape and size of leaf: needle or spine, graminoid, medium or small, broad, compound, and thalloid
(5) Leaf texture: filmy, membranous, sclerophyll, succulent, and fungoid
(6) Coverage: barren or very sparse, discontinuous, in tufts or groups, and continuous

This system has been used in comparing and contrasting vegetation in different regions and in various stages of succession. Finally it may be added that wide use has been made of physiognomic classification in depicting vegetation types on maps.[131]

Geographical Characteristics

Communities may be classified on the basis of geographical distribution (synchorology), in which various terms such as regional vegetation types, formations, zones, and belts are used (Figures 1-1 and 5-2). Physiognomy is the chief characteristic employed, but other criteria, including species composition and habitat, may also be used. For example, Schimper and von Faber[176] classified the vegetation of the world into 15 formations, namely: tropical rainforest, monsoon forest, temperate rainforest, summer-green deciduous forest, needleleaf forest, evergreen hardwood forest, savanna woodland, thorn forest and scrub, savanna, half desert, heath, dry desert, tundra, cold woodland, and cold desert. Another example is Dice's classification,[69] in which North America was divided into 28 biotic provinces, each characterized by peculiarities of vegetation type, ecological climax, flora, fauna, climate, physiography, and soil. The biotic provinces were subdivided into biotic districts and life belts; and ecologic associations below the rank of life belt were considered as relatively stable communities.

The major plant-animal formations, or "biociations," in North America have been classified and mapped by Kendeigh[124] into tundra, alpine meadow, boreal forest-edge, boreal forest, western forest, prairie, woodland, chaparral, basin sagebrush, desert scrub, deciduous forest, deciduous forest-edge, and southern pine. The biociations are further divided into plant-animal communities. In this hierarchical system, criteria of floristics, faunistics, plant and animal sociology, and community dynamics are used.

According to Knapp[127] the chief formations or "zones" of Europe (excluding the extreme southern, southeastern, and western parts) are the evergreen-sclerophyllous-woody vegetation near the Mediterranean; the *Quercus pubescens* formation in southern Europe, extending from Spain to the Balkans; the *Quercus-Carpinus* mixed forest, extending from England to east-central Europe, north to southern Scandinavia, and southeast to the Balkans; the mountain-beech forest reaching from northeastern Spain to the Carpathian and Balkan mountains; the spruce forest at higher elevations in the mountains in central and southeastern Europe, but most widespread in Fennoscandinavia and northeastern Europe; the *Empetrum* "zone," containing open woods and dwarf shrubs at high elevations with a distribution similar to the preceding; and the arctic-alpine "zone" above the tree-line in the mountains, and north to the tree-line in the higher latitudes.

Zonal classification of vegetation in restricted regions is useful. As an example, the plant life of the Rocky Mountains has been classified by Daubenmire[65] into six major zones: alpine tundra, Engelmann spruce-alpine fir, Douglas fir, ponderosa pine, juniper-pinyon, and oak-mountain mahogany. Another example has been described on the east coast of Greenland,[83] where the common zonation from the sea to the uplands comprises communities of *Festuca rubra* nearest the sea, followed by those of *Cassiope tetragona, Vaccinium uliginosum,* and *Dryas integrifolium,* and, farthest from the sea, the lichen-moss assemblages. The complex gradient from the sea to the uplands shows decreasing depth of snow cover and increasing exposure to winds in the winter.

CONCLUSION

It may be concluded that while all the various kinds of classification of vegetation have value, the kind to employ is determined by the purpose or need of the investigator, the extensiveness of the area, and the available time and facilities. When one starts with a large area, the geographic, physiognomic, and ecologic criteria are the most useful. The resulting units may be subdivided by the same criteria, but final classification of the fundamental units, based on their own intrinsic properties, requires the use of floristic composition, particularly the kinds and numbers of species, as well as dominant, constant, and characteristic species. Classification based on the kind of succession and the stage in the sere, in order to be adequate, must be accompanied by floristic analysis and description of all the communities making up the various stages. Classification, however, when analytic data on intrinsic properties and descriptions are available, may begin with the basic units, which are usually small in area and homogeneous. In any case, whether one is primarily concerned with geographic distribution, physiognomy, habitat conditions, successional sequences, or plant sociological analysis, a comprehensive and satisfying classification must include consideration of the properties of the stands, and these properties can only be revealed by detailed analysis.

GENERAL REFERENCES

Becking, R. W., "The Zürich-Montpellier School of Phytosociology," *Botan. Rev.*, **23**, 411–488 (1957).

Braun-Blanquet, J., "Plant Sociology," McGraw-Hill Book Co., New York, N.Y., 1932.

Conard, H. S., "The Vegetation of Iowa," *Univ. Iowa Stud. Ser.*, **19**, No. 424, 1–166 (1952).

Knapp, R., "Arbeitsmethoden der Pflanzensoziologie und Eigenschaften der Pflanzengesellschaften, I. Einführung in die Pflanzensoziologie," Eugen Ulmer, Stuttgart, Germany, 1958.

Poore, M.E.D., "The Use of Phytosociological Methods in Ecological Investigations, I. The Braun-Blanquet System," *Jour. Ecol.*, **43**, 226–244 (1955); "II. Practical Issues Involved in an Attempt to Apply the Braun-Blanquet System," *Ibid.*, **43**, 245–269 (1955); "III. Practical Application," *Ibid.*, **43**, 606–651 (1955); "IV. General Discussion of Phytosociological Problems," *Ibid.*, **44**, 28–50 (1956).

Weaver, J. E. and Clements, F. E., "Plant Ecology," 2nd Ed., McGraw-Hill Book Co., New York, N.Y., 1938.

Whittaker, R. H., "Recent Evolution of Ecological Concepts in Relation to the Eastern Forests of North America," pp. 340–358 *in* "Fifty Years of Botany," W. C. Steere, Ed., McGraw-Hill Book Co., New York, N.Y., 1958.

BIBLIOGRAPHY

1. Alechin, W.W., "Die vegetationsanalystischen Methoden der Moskauer Steppenforscher," *Abderhalden Handb. Biol. Arbeitsmethoden,* Lief. 379, **XI,** Teil 6, 335–373 (1932).
2. Allee, W.C., Emerson, A.E., Park, O., Park, T., and Schmidt, K.P., "Principles of Animal Ecology," W. B. Saunders Co., Philadelphia, 1949.
3. Anderson, E., "Introgressive Hybridization," John Wiley & Sons, Inc., New York, N.Y., 1949.
4. Anderson, E., "Man as a Maker of New Plants and New Plant Communities," pp. 763–777 *in* Thomas, W.L., "Man's Role in Changing the Face of the Earth," Univ. Chicago Press, Chicago, Ill., 1956.
5. Anderson, N.L. and Wright, J.C., "Grasshopper Investigations on Montana Range Lands," *Montana Agric. Expt. Sta. Bull.,* No. 486, 1–46 (1952).
6. Anderson, S.R. and Metcalf, D.S., "Seed Yields of Birdsfoot Trefoil (*Lotus corniculatus* L.), as Affected by Pre-harvest Clipping and by Growing in Association with Three Adapted Grasses," *Agron. Jour.,* **49,** 52–55 (1957).
7. Anderson, W.A., "Development of Prairie at Iowa Lakeside Laboratory," *Am. Midland Naturalist,* **36,** 431–455 (1946).
8. Ashby, E., "Statistical Ecology. II. A Reassessment," *Botan. Rev.,* **14,** 222–234 (1948).
9. Backlund, H.O., "Red Locusts and Vegetation," *Oikos,* **6,** 124–148 (1955).
10. Beadle, N.C.W., "The Misuse of Climate as an Indicator of Vegetation and Soils," *Ecology,* **32,** 343–345 (1951).
11. Becking, R.W., "The Zürich-Montpellier School of Phytosociology," *Botan. Rev.,* **23,** 411–488 (1957).
12. Bess, H.A. and Haramoto, F.H., "Biological Control of Pamakini, *Eupatorium adenophorum,* in Hawaii by a Tephritid Gall Fly, *Procecidochares utilis.* 2. Population Studies of the Fly," *Ecology,* **40,** 244–249 (1959).
13. Billings, W.D., "Vegetation and Plant Growth as Affected by Chemically Altered Rocks in the Western Great Basin," *Ecology,* **31,** 62–74 (1950).
14. Billings, W.D., "The Environmental Complex in Relation to Plant Growth and Distribution," *Quart. Rev. Biol.,* **27,** 251–264 (1952).
15. Biswell, H.H., "Ecology of California Grasslands," *Jour. Range Management,* **9,** 19–24 (1956).
15A. Blaisdell, J.P., "Seasonal Development and Yield of Native Plants on the Upper Snake River Plains and Their Relation to Certain Climatic Factors," *U. S. Dept. Agric. Tech. Bull.,* No. 1190, 1–68 (1958).

16. Blake, S. T., "The Plant Communities of Western Queensland and Their Relationships, with Special Reference to the Grazing Industry," *Proc. Roy. Soc. Queensland*, **49**, 146–204 (1938).

17. Boatman, D.J., *"Mercurialis perennis* L. in Ireland," *Jour. Ecol.*, **44**, 587–596 (1956).

18. Böcher, T.W., "Oceanic and Continental Vegetational Complexes in Southwest Greenland," *Medd. Gronland*, **148**, No. 1, 1–336 (1954).

19. Bonner, J., "The Role of Toxic Substances in the Interaction of Higher Plants," *Botan. Rev.*, **16**, 51–64 (1950).

20. Bonner, J., "Chemical Sociology Among the Plants," pp. 156–162 *in* "Plant Life, a Scientific American Book," Simon & Schuster, Inc., New York, N.Y., 1957.

21. Bourdeau, P.F. and Oosting, H.J., "The Maritime Live-oak Forest in North Carolina," *Ecology*, **40**, 148–152 (1959).

22. Braun, E.Lucy, "Deciduous Forests of North America," Blakiston & Co., Philadelphia, 1950.

23. Braun, E.Lucy, "The Development of Association and Climax Concepts: Their Use in Interpretation of the Deciduous Forest," *Am. Jour. Botany*, **43**, 906–911 (1956).

24. Braun-Blanquet,J., "Plant Sociology," McGraw-Hill Book Co., New York, N.Y., 1932.

25. Braun-Blanquet, J., "Pflanzensoziologie. Grundzüge der Vegetation-skunde," 2nd Ed., Springer-Verlag, Vienna, 1951.

26. Braun-Blanquet, J., Pallman, H., and Bach, R., "Pflanzensoziologie und Bodenkundliche Untersuchungen in Schweizerischen Nationalpark und seinen Nachbargebieten. II. Vegetation und Böden der Wald- und Zwergstrauchgesellscahften (Vaccinio-Picetalia)," *Ergeb. wissensch. schweiz. Nationalparks*, **IV** (N.F.), No. 28 (1954).

27. Brown, Dorothy, "Methods of Surveying and Measuring Vegetation," *Commonwealth Bur. Pastures and Field Crops Bull.*, No. 42, 1–223 (1954).

28. Buell, M.F. and Wilbur, R.L. "Life-form Spectra of the Hardwood Forests of the Itasca Park Region, Minnesota," *Ecology*, **29**, 352–359 (1948).

29. Burton, G.W., "Quantitative Inheritance in Grasses," *Proc. 6th Intern. Grassland Congr.*, Pennsylvania State College, 1952.

30. Buzzati-Traverso, A.A., "Populations in Time and Space: Synthesis," *Cold Spring Harbor Symposia Quant. Biol.*, **20**, 300–302 (1955).

31. Cain, S.A. and Castro, G.M.DeO., "Manual of Vegetation Analysis," Harper & Bros., New York, N.Y., 1959.

32. Cain, S.A., Nelson, Mary, and McLean, W., "Andropogonetum Hemp-steadii: a Long Island Grassland Vegetation Type," *Am. Midland Naturalist*, **18**, 324–350 (1937).

33. Cajander, A.K., "The Theory of Forest Types," *Acta-forestalia Fennica*, **29**, 1–108 (1926).

34. Campbell, R.S., "Plant Succession and Grazing Capacity on Clay Soils in Southern New Mexico," *Jour. Agri. Research*, **43**, 1027–1051 (1931).

35. Canfield, R.H., "Perennial Grass Composition as an Indicator of Condition of Southwestern Mixed Grass Ranges," *Ecology*, **29**, 190–204 (1948).

36. Carter, J.F. and Ahlgren, H.L., "Forage Yields and Disease Development of Two Varieties of Smooth Bromegrass, *Bromus inermis* Leyss., Grown Under Various Conditions in the Field," *Agron. Jour.*, **43**, 166–171 (1951).

37. Chapin, W.E., Hafenrichter, A.L., and Law, A.G., "Performance of Strains of *Lotus corniculatus* on the North Pacific Coast," *Agron. Jour.*, **43**, 438–442 (1951).

38. Chapman, V.J., "Salt Marshes and Ecological Terminology," *Vegetatio*, **8**, 215–234 (1959).

39. Churchill, E.D. and Hanson, H.C., "The Concept of Climax in Arctic and Alpine Vegetation," *Botan. Rev.*, **24**, 127–191 (1958).

40. Clausen, J., Keck, D.D., and Hiesey, W.M., "Experimental Studies on the Nature of Species. II. Plant Evolution Through Amphiploidy and Autoploidy, with Examples from Madiinae," *Carnegie Inst. Washington Publ.*, No. 564 (1945).

41. Clements, F.E., "Plant Succession," *Carnegie Inst. Wash. Publ.*, No. 242 (1916).

42. Clements, F.E., "Plant Succession and Indicators; a Definitive Edition of Plant Succession and Plant Indicators," H. W. Wilson Co., New York, N.Y., 1928.

43. Clements, F.E. and Shelford, V.E., "Bio-ecology," John Wiley & Sons, Inc., New York, N.Y., 1939.

44. Clements, F.E., Weaver, J.E., and Hanson, H.C., "Plant Competition," *Carnegie Inst. Wash. Publ.*, No. 398 (1929).

45. Cole, LaMont C., "Sketches of General and Comparative Demography," pp. 1–15 *in* "Population Studies: Animal Ecology and Demography," *Cold Spring Harbor Symposia Quant. Biol.*, **22** (1957).

46. Conard, H.S., "The Plant Associations of Central Long Island," *Am. Midland Naturalist*, **16**, 433–516 (1935).

47. Conard, H.S., "The Background of Plant Ecology" (translated from the German of Kerner, A., 1863, "The Plant Life of the Danube Basin"), Iowa State Coll. Press, Ames, Iowa, 1951.

48. Conard, H.S., "The Vegetation of Iowa," *Univ. Iowa Study Ser.*, **19**, No. 424, 1–166 (1952).

49. Conard, H.S., "Phylogeny and Ontogeny in Plant Sociology," *Vegetatio*, **5–6**, 11–15 (1954).

50. Cooke, W.B., "Soil Fungi in Relation to Root Disease," *Ecology*, **37**, 857–858 (1956).

51. Coombe, D.E. and Frost, L.C., "The Heaths of the Cornish Serpentine," *Jour. Ecology*, **44**, 226–256 (1956).

52. Coombe, D.E. and White, F., "Notes on Calcicolous Communities and Peat Formation in Norwegian Lappland," *Jour. Ecol.*, **39**, 33–62 (1951).

53. Cooper, W.S., "The Fundamentals of Vegetational Change," *Ecology*, **7**, 391–413 (1926).
54. Cooper, W.C., "A Third Expedition to Glacier Bay, Alaska," *Ecology*, **12**, 61–95 (1931).
55. Cooper, W.S., "A Fourth Expedition to Glacier Bay, Alaska," *Ecology*, **20**, 130–155 (1939).
56. Costello, D.F. and Price, R., "Weather and Plant Development Data as Determinants of Grazing Periods on Mountain Range," *U. S. Dept. Agric. Tech. Bull.*, No. 686, 1–30 (1939).
57. Coupland, R.T., "Ecology of the Mixed Prairie in Canada," *Ecol. Monographs*, **20**, 271–315 (1950).
58. Cowles, H.C., "The Causes of Vegetative Cycles," *Botan. Gaz.*, **51**, 161–183 (1911).
59. Craddock, G.W. and Forsling, C.I., "The Influence of Climate and Grazing on Spring-Fall Sheep Range in Southeastern Idaho," *U. S. Dept. Agric. Tech. Bull.*, No. 600, 1–42 (1938).
60. Curtis, J.T., "A Prairie Continuum in Wisconsin," *Ecology*, **36**, 558–566 (1955).
61. Dahl, E., "Biogeographic and Geologic Indications of Unglaciated Areas in Scandinavia During the Glacial Ages," *Bull. Geol. Soc. Am.*, **66**, 1499–1519 (1955).
62. Dahl, E., "Rondane, Mountain Vegetation in South Norway and Its Relation to the Environment," Aschehoug & Co., Oslo, 1956.
63. Dansereau, P., "Description and Recording of Vegetation Upon a Structural Basis," *Ecology*, **32**, 172–229 (1951).
64. Daubenmire, R.F., "Plant Succession Due to Overgrazing in the *Agropyron* Bunchgrass Prairie in Southeastern Washington," *Ecology*, **21**, 55–64 (1940).
65. Daubenmire, R.F., "Vegetational Zonation in the Rocky Mountains," *Botan. Rev.*, **9**, 325–393 (1943).
66. Daubenmire, R.F., "Forest Vegetation of Northern Idaho and Adjacent Washington, and Its Bearing on Concepts of Vegetation Classification," *Ecol. Monographs*, **22**, 301–330 (1952).
67. Daubenmire, R.F., "Plants and Environment, a Textbook of Plant Autecology," 2nd Ed., John Wiley & Sons, Inc., New York, N.Y., 1959.
68. Dempster, E.R., "Maintenance of Genetic Heterogeneity," *Cold Spring Harbor Symposia Quant. Biol.*, **20**, 25–32 (1955).
69. Dice, L.R., "The Biotic Provinces of North America," Univ. Michigan Press, Ann Arbor, Mich., 1943.
70. Dice, L.R., "Natural Communities," Univ. Michigan Press, Ann Arbor, Mich., 1952.
70A. Dotzenko, A.D. and Stegmeier, W.D., "Pollen Shedding in Russian Wildrye Grass," *Agron. Jour.*, **51**, 594–595 (1959).
71. Drew, W.B., "Floristic Composition of Grazed and Ungrazed Prairie Vegetation in North-central Missouri," *Ecology*, **28**, 26–41 (1947).

72. Drury, W.H.,Jr., "Bog Flats and Physiographic Processes in the Upper Kuskokwim River Region, Alaska," *Contribs. Gray Herbarium,* **178,** 1–130 (1956).

73. Eberhart, S.A. and Newell, L.C., "Variation in Domestic Collections of Switchgrass, *Panicum virgatum* L.," *Agron. Jour.,* **51,** 613–616 (1959).

74. Egler, F.E., "Vegetation as an Object of Study," *Philosophy of Science,* **9,** 245–260 (1942).

75. Ellenberg, H., "Landwirtschaftliche Pflanzensoziologie. I. Unkrautgemeinschaften als Zeiger für Klima und Boden," Eugen Ulmer, Stuttgart, 1950.

76. Ellenberg, H., "Landwirtschaftliche Pflanzensoziologie. II. Wiesen und Weiden und ihre standörtliche Bewertung," Eugen Ulmer, Stuttgart, 1952.

77. Ellison, L., "Subalpine Vegetation of the Wastch Plateau, Utah," *Ecol. Monographs,* **24,** 89–184 (1954).

78. Faegri, K., "Some Recent Publications on Phytogeography in Scandinavia, *Botan. Rev.,* **3,** 425–456 (1937).

79. Faegri, K., "Norges Planter," Cappelens Forlag, Oslo, 1958.

80. Ford, E.B., "Rapid Evolution and the Conditions Which Make It Possible," *Cold Spring Harbor Symposia Quant. Biol.,* **20,** 230–238 (1955).

81. Fries, Th. C.E., "Botanische Untersuchungen 1910–1913 im nördlichsten Schweden, *Flora och Fauna,* **2** (1913).

82. Gates, D.H. and Harris, G.A., "Longevity, Competitive Ability, and Productivity of Grasses in Three Northeastern Washington Nurseries," *Northwest Sci.,* **33,** 76–83 (1959).

83. Gelting, P., "A West Greenland *Dryas integrifolia* Community Rich in Lichens," *Svensk Botan. Tidskr.,* **49,** 295–313 (1955).

84. Gillham, Mary E., "Ecology of the Pembrokeshire Islands. V. Manuring by the Colonial Seabirds and Mammals, with a Note on Seed Distribution by Gulls," *Jour. Ecol.,* **44,** 429–454 (1956).

85. Gimingham, C.H. and Robertson, E.T., "Preliminary Investigations on the Structure of Bryophytic Communities," *Trans. Brit. Bryol. Soc.,* **1,** 330–344 (1950).

86. Gjaerevoll, O., "The Snow-bed Vegetation in the Surroundings of Lake Torneträsk, Swedish Lappland," *Svensk Botan. Tidskr.,* **44,** 387–440 (1950).

87. Gjaerevoll, O., "Botanikk og Vegbygging i Høgfjellet," from "Syn og Segn," pp. 1–8, Oslo, 1952.

88. Gleason, H.A., "Further Views on the Succession Concept," *Ecology,* **8,** 299–326 (1927).

89. Gleason, H.A., "Is the Synusia an Association?" *Ecology,* **17,** 444–451 (1936).

90. Gleason, H.A., "The Individualistic Concept of the Plant Association," *Am. Midland Naturalist,* **21,** 92–110 (1939).

91. Godwin, H., "The Sub-climax and Deflected Succession," *Jour. Ecol.*, **17**, 144–147 (1929).

92. Good, R., "The Geography of Flowering Plants," 2nd Ed., Longmans, Green & Co., London, 1953.

93. Goodall, D.W., "Objective Methods for the Classification of Vegetation. I. The Use of Positive Interspecific Correlation," *Australian Jour. Botan.*, **1**, 39–63 (1953); II. "Fidelity and Indicator Value," *Ibid.*, **1**, 434–456 (1953); III. "An Essay in the Use of Factor Analysis," *Ibid.*, **2**, 304–324 (1954).

94. Graham, B.F.,Jr., "Transfer of Dye Through Natural Root Grafts of *Pinus strobus* L.," *Ecology*, **41**, 56–64 (1960).

95. Greig-Smith, P., "Quantitative Plant Ecology," Academic Press, Inc., New York, N.Y., 1957.

96. Grunder, M.S. and Dermanis, P., "The Effect of Pollinator Plants on Seed Set in Vegetatively Propagated Orchard Grass," *Agron. Jour.*, **44**, 275–276 (1952).

97. Haftorn, S., "Synzoisk Fröspredning hos Norske Fugler," *Blyttia*, **14**, 103–121 (1956).

98. Hanson, A.A. and Carnahan, H.L., "Breeding Perennial Forage Grasses," *U. S. Dept. Agric. Tech. Bull.*, No. 1145, 1–116 (1956).

99. Hanson, Herbert C., "Ecology of the Grassland, II," *Botan. Rev.*, **16**, 283–360 (1950).

100. Hanson, Herbert C., "Vegetation Types in Northwestern Alaska and Comparisons with Communities in Other Arctic Regions," *Ecology*, **34**, 111–140 (1953).

101. Hanson, Herbert C., "Characteristics of the *Stipa comata-Bouteloua gracilis-Bouteloua curtipendula* Association of Northern Colorado," *Ecology*, **36**, 269–280 (1955).

102. Hanson, H.C. and Ball, W.S., "An Application of Raunkiaer's Law of Frequency to Grazing Studies," *Ecology*, **9**, 467–473 (1928).

103. Hanson, H.C. and Dahl, E., "Some Grassland Communities in the Mountain-front Zone in Northern Colorado," *Vegetatio*, **7**, 249–270 (1957).

104. Hanson, H.C. and Love, L.D., "Size of List Quadrat for Use in Determining the Effects of Different Systems of Grazing upon *Agropyron smithii* Mixed Prairie," *Jour. Agr. Research*, **41**, 549–560 (1930).

105. Hanson, H.C., Love, L.D., and Morris, M.S., "Effects of Different Systems of Grazing by Cattle upon a Western Wheat-grass Type of Range," *Colo. Agr. Exp. Sta. Bull.*, No. 377, 1–82 (1931).

106. Hanson, H.C. and Whitman, W., "Characteristics of Major Grassland Types in Western North Dakota," *Ecol. Monographs*, **8**, 57–114 (1938).

107. Hardison, J.R., "Seed Disorders of Forage Plants," *U. S. Dept. Agr. Yearbook, Plant Diseases*, 272–276, 1953.

108. Haskell, G., "Analyses of Sexual-apomictic Blackberry Populations and Their Ecological Consequences," *Cold Spring Harbor Symposia Quant. Biol.*, **20**, 111–126 (1955).

109. Heslop-Harrison, J., "New Concepts in Flowering-plant Taxonomy," Harvard Univ. Press, Cambridge, Mass., 1956.

110. Holmgren, R.C., "Competition Between Annuals and Young Bitterbrush (*Purshia tridentata*) in Idaho," *Ecology,* **37,** 370–377 (1956).

111. Holscher, C.E., "The Effects of Clipping Bluestem Wheatgrass and Blue Grama at Different Heights and Frequencies," *Ecology,* **26,** 148–156 (1945).

112. Hulburt, L.C., "Ecological Studies of *Bromus tectorum* and Other Annual Bromegrasses," *Ecol. Monographs,* **25,** 181–213 (1955).

113. Hull, A.C., Jr. and Stewart, G., "Replacing Cheatgrass by Reseeding with Perennial Grass on Southern Idaho Ranges," *Jour. Am. Soc. Agron.,* **40,** 694–703 (1948).

113A. Iaroshenko, P.D., "On Changes in the Plant Cover," *Bot. Zhurnal. SSSR,* **31,** 29–40 (1946).

114. Iverson, J., "Biologische Pflanzentypen als Hilfsmittel in der Vegetationsforschung," Munksgaard, Copenhagen, 1936.

115. Johnson, C.G., "The Study of Wind-borne Insect Populations in Relation to Terrestrial Ecology, Flight Periodicity and the Estimation of Aerial Populations," *Scien. Prog.,* **39,** 41–62 (1951).

116. Johnson, W.M., "Natural Revegetation of Abandoned Crop Land in the Ponderosa Pine Zone of the Pike's Peak Region in Colorado," *Ecology,* **26,** 363–374 (1945).

117. Johnson, W.M., "Effect of Grazing Intensity Upon Vegetation and Cattle Gains on Ponderosa Pine-Bunchgrass Ranges of the Front Range of Colorado," *U. S. Dept. Agric. Circ.,* No. 929, 1–36 (1953).

118. Johnson, W.M., "The Effect of Grazing Intensity on Plant Composition, Vigor, and Growth of Pine-Bunchgrass Ranges in Central Colorado," *Ecology,* **37,** 790–798 (1956).

119. Jones, M.D. and Newell, L.C., "Size, Variability, and Identification of Grass Pollen," *Jour. Am. Soc. Agron.,* **40,** 136–143 (1946).

120. Juhren, M., Went, F.W., and Phillips, E., "Ecology of Desert Plants. IV. Combined Field and Laboratory Work on Germination of Annuals in the Joshua Tree National Monument, California," *Ecology,* **37,** 318–330 (1956).

121. Katz, N.J., "Sphagnum Bogs of Central Russia: Phytosociology, Ecology, and Succession," *Jour. Ecol.,* **14,** 177–202 (1926).

122. Keever, Catherine, "Causes of Succession on Old Fields of the Piedmont, North Carolina," *Ecol. Monographs,* **20,** 228–250 (1950).

123. Kellogg, C.E., "Morphology and Genesis of the Solonetz Soils of Western North Dakota," *Soil Sci.,* **38,** 483–501 (1934).

124. Kendeigh, S.C., "History and Evaluation of Various Concepts of Plant and Animal Communities in North America," *Ecology,* **35,** 152–171 (1954).

125. Kershaw, K.A., "The Use of Cover and Frequency in the Detection of Pattern in Plant Communities," *Ecology,* **38,** 291–299 (1957).

126. Kershaw, K.A., "An Investigation of the Structure of a Grassland Community. I. The Pattern of *Agrostis tenuis*," *Jour. Ecol.*, **46,** 571–592 (1958); "II. The Pattern of *Dactylis glomerata, Lolium perenne,* and *Trifolium repens,* III. Discussion and Conclusions," *Ibid.*, **47,** 31–53 (1959).

127. Knapp, R., "Arbeitsmethoden der Pflanzensoziologie und Eigenschaften der Pflanzengesellschaften, I. Einführung in die Pflanzensoziologie," Eugen Ulmer, Stuttgart, 1958.

128. Koller, D., "Germination-regulating Mechanisms in Some Desert Seeds. III. *Calligonum comosum* L'Her.," *Ecology,* **37,** 430–433 (1956).

129. Kreitlow, K.W. and Juska, F.V., "Susceptibility of Merion and Other Kentucky Bluegrass Varieties to Stripe Smut (*Ustilago striiformis*)," *Agron. Jour.,* **51,** 596–597 (1959).

130. Kreitzinger, E.J., Fischer, G.W., and Law, A.S., "Reaction of Mountain Brome and Canada Wildrye Strains to Head Smut (*Ustilago bullata* Berk.)," *Jour. Agr. Research,* **75,** 105–111 (1947).

131. Küchler, A.W., "A Physiognomic Classification of Vegetation," *Annals Asso. Am. Geog.,* **39,** 201–210 (1949).

132. Larson, F. and Whitman, W., "A Comparison of Used and Unused Grassland Mesas in the Badlands of South Dakota," *Ecology,* **23,** 438–445 (1942).

133. Lawrence, W.E., "Some Ecotypic Relations of *Deschampsia caespitosa*," *Am. Jour. Botany,* **32,** 298–314 (1945).

134. Lems, K., "Botanical Notes on the Canary Islands. I. Introgression Among the Species of Adenocarpus and Their Role in the Vegetation of the Islands," *Inst. Nacional Invest. Agron.* (Spain), **276,** 351–370 (1958).

135. Lewontin, R., "The Effects of Population Density and Composition on Viability in *Drosophila melanogaster*," *Evolution,* **9,** 27–41 (1955).

136. Lindeman, R.L., "The Trophic-Dynamic Aspect of Ecology," *Ecology,* **23,** 399–418 (1942).

137. Lommasson, T. and Jensen, C., "Determining Utilization of Range Grasses from Height-Weight Tables," *Jour. Forestry,* **41,** 589–593 (1943).

138. Lynch, D., "Ecology of the Aspen Groveland in Glacier County, Montana," *Ecology,* **25,** 321–344 (1955).

138A. McCarty, E.C., "The Relation of Growth to the Varying Carbohydrate Content in Mountain Brome," *U. S. Dept. Agric. Tech. Bull.,* No. 598, 1–24 (1938).

139. McDougall, W.B., "Plant Ecology," 4th Ed., Lea & Febiger, Philadelphia, Pa., 1949.

140. McMillan, C., "Nature of the Grassland Type of Community," pp. 325–331 *in* "Grasslands," Am. Assoc. Advance. Sci., Washington, D.C., 1959.

141. McMillan, C., "The Role of Ecotypic Variation in the Distribution of the Central Grassland of North America," *Ecol. Monographs,* **29,** 285–308 (1959).

142. Major, J., "A Functional Factorial Approach to Plant Ecology," *Ecology,* **32,** 392–412 (1951).

143. Martin, N.D., "An Analysis of Forest Succession in Algonquin Park, Ontario," *Ecol. Monographs,* **29,** 187–218 (1959).

144. Martin, W.E., "The Vegetation of Island Beach State Park, New Jersey," *Ecol. Monographs,* **29,** 1–46 (1959).

145. Mayr, E., "Integration of Genotypes: Synthesis," *Cold Spring Harbor Symposia Quant. Biol.,* **20,** 326–333 (1955).

146. Mazurak, A.P. and Conard, E.C., "Rates of Water Entry in the Three Great Soil Groups After Seven Years in Grasses and Small Grains," *Agron. Jour.,* **51,** 264–267 (1959).

147. Metcalfe, G., "The Ecology of the Cairngorms. Part II. The Mountain Callunetum," *Jour. Ecol.,* **38,** 46–74 (1950).

148. Moore, C.W.E., "The Competitive Effect of *Danthonia* spp. on the Establishment of *Bothriochloa ambigua,*" *Ecology,* **40,** 141–143 (1959).

149. Mothes, K., "Physiology of the Alkaloids," *Ann. Rev. Plant Physiol.,* **6,** 393–432 (1955).

150. Nicholson, A.J., "The Self-adjustment of Populations to Change," *Cold Spring Harbor Symposia Quant. Biol.,* **22,** 153–173 (1957).

151. Nordhagen, R., "Sikilsdalen og Norges Fjellbeiter. En Plantesosiologisk Monografi," John Grieg, Bergen (1943).

152. Nuttonson, M.Y., "The Role of Bioclimatology in Agriculture with Special Reference to the Use of Thermal and Photo-thermal Requirements of Pure-line Varieties of Plants as a Biological Indicator in Ascertaining Climatic Analogues (Homoclimes)," *Intern. Jour. Bioclim. and Biometeorol.,* I (**II,**B2), 1–8 (1957).

153. Nytzenko, A.A., "Boundaries of Plant Associations in Nature" (Russian), *Bot. Zhurnal SSSR,* **33,** 487–495 (1948); *Biol. Absts.,* **24,** 17407 (1950).

154. Oberlander, G.T., "Summer Fog Precipitation on the San Francisco Peninsula," *Ecology,* **37,** 851–852 (1956).

155. Odum, E.P., "Fundamentals of Ecology," 2nd Ed., W. B. Saunders Co., Philadelphia, Pa., 1959.

156. Olmsted, C.E., "Growth and Development in Range Grasses. V. Photoperiodic Responses of Clonal Divisions of Three Latitudinal Strains of Side-oats Grama," *Botan. Gaz.,* **106,** 382–401 (1945).

157. Oosting, H.J. and Reed, J.F., "Virgin Spruce-Fir Forest in the Medicine Bow Mountains, Wyoming," *Ecol. Monographs,* **22,** 69–91 (1952).

158. Ovington, J.D., "Studies of the Development of Woodland Conditions under Different Trees. V. The Mineral Composition of the Ground Flora," *Jour. Ecol.,* **44,** 597–604 (1956).

159. Paczoski, J.K., "Vegetationsbeschreibung des Gouv. Cherson. II. Die Steppen Cherson" (1917), (trans. from the Russian, and referred to by Alechin, W. W., *in* "Was ist eine Pflanzengesellschaft: Ihr Wesen und ihr Wert als Ausdruck des sozialen Lebens des Pflanzen," *Fedde Reprt. specs. nowar. reg. veg. Beih,* **37,** 1–50 (1926)). *In* Cain, S. A., "The Climax and Its Complexities," *Am. Midland Naturalist,* **21,** 146–181 (1939).

160. Penfound, W.T., "A Phytosociological Analysis of a Goldenrod Community Near Kenner, Louisiana," *Ecology,* **29,** 124–125 (1948).

161. Phillips, J., "Agriculture and Ecology in Africa. A Study of Actual and Potential Development South of the Sahara," F. A. Praeger, New York, N.Y., 1960.

162. Piemeisel, R.L., "Replacement Control: Changes in Vegetation in Relation to Control of Pests and Diseases," *Botan. Rev.,* **20,** 1–32 (1954).

163. Pigott, C.D., "The Vegetation of Upper Teesdale in the North Pennines," *Jour. Ecol.,* **44,** 545–586 (1956).

164. Pitelka, F.A., "Some Characteristics of Microtine Cycles in the Arctic," pp. 73–88 *in* "Arctic Biology," *Biol. Colloq. Proc.,* Oregon State College (1957).

165. Polunin, N., "The Vegetation of Akpatok Island. I–II." *Jour. Ecol.,* **22,** 337–395; **23,** 161–209 (1934–1935).

166. Poore, M.E.D., "The Use of Phytosociological Methods in Ecological Investigations. I. The Braun-Blanquet System," *Jour. Ecol.,* **43,** 226–244 (1955); "II. Practical Issues Involved in an Attempt to Apply the Braun-Blanquet System," *Ibid.,* **43,** 245–269 (1955); "III. Practical Application," *Ibid.,* **43,** 606–651 (1955); "IV. General Discussion of Phytosociological Problems," *Ibid.,* **44,** 28–50 (1956).

167. Poore, M.E.D. and McVean, D.N., "A New Approach to Scottish Mountain Vegetation," *Jour. Ecol.,* **45,** 401–439 (1957).

168. Ramaley, F., "Xerophytic Grasslands at Different Altitudes in Colorado," *Bull. Torrey Botan. Club,* **46,** 37–52 (1919).

169. Raunkiaer, C., "The Life Forms of Plants and Statistical Plant Geography, Being the Collected Papers of C. Raunkiaer," Clarendon Press, Oxford, 1934.

169A. Reynolds, H.G., "Managing Grass-Shrub Cattle Ranges in the Southwest," *U. S. Dept. Agric. Handbook,* No. 162, 1–40 (1959).

170. Richards, P.W., "Ecological Studies on the Rain Forest of Southern Nigeria. I. The Structure and Floristic Composition of the Primary Forest," *Jour. Ecol.,* **27,** 1–61 (1939).

171. Richards, P.W., "The Tropical Rain Forest," Cambridge Univ. Press, Cambridge, 1952.

172. Ridley, H.N., "The Dispersal of Plants Throughout the World," Reeve & Co., Ltd., Ashford, Kent, 1930.

173. Robertson, J.H., "Responses of Range Grasses to Different Intensities of Competition with Sagebrush (*Artemisia tridentata* Nutt.)," *Ecology,* **28,** 1–16 (1947).

174. Rønning, O., "Noen Høydegrenser for Planter paa Spitsbergen," *Blyttia,* **17,** 53–60 (1959).

175. Savage, D.A., "The Line-transect Method, an Improved Method of Studying Native Range Vegetation," *U. S. Dept. Agric. Mimeo. Leaflet* (1940).

176. Schimper, A.F.W. and Von Faber, F.C., "Pflanzen geographie auf Physiologischer Grundlage," Aufl. 3, Gustav Fischer, Jena, 1935.

177. Selander, S., "Floristic Phytogeography of Southwestern Lule Lappmark (Swedish Lapland)," *Acta Geog. Suecica,* **27,** 1–200 (1950).

178. Shreve, E.B., "Seasonal Changes in the Water Relations of Desert Plants," *Ecology,* **4,** 266–292 (1923).

179. Shreve, F., "Vegetation of the Sonoran Desert," *Carnegie Inst. Wash. Publ.,* No. 591, 1951.

180. Silliman, F.E. and Leisner, R.S., "An Analysis of a Colony of Hybrid Oaks," *Amer. Jour. Botany,* **45,** 730–736 (1958).

180A. Sörensen, Th., "A Method of Establishing Groups of Equal Amplitude in Plant Sociology Based on Similarity of Species Content," *Kgl. Danske Videnskab. Selskab Biol. Skrifter,* **J5,** No. 4, 1–34 (1948).

181. Sprague, V.G. and Garber, R.J., "Effect of Time and Height of Cutting and Nitrogen Fertilization on the Persistence of the Legume and Production of Orchardgrass-Ladino and Bromegrass-Ladino Associations," *Agron. Jour.,* **42,** 586–593 (1950).

182. Stebbins, G.L., "Species Hybrids in Grasses," *Proc. Internat. Grassl. Cong.,* I, 247–253, Pennsylvania State College, 1952.

183. Stebbins, G.L., "Cytogenetics and Evolution of the Grass Family," *Amer. Jour. Botany,* **43,** 890–905 (1956).

184. Steere, W.C., "The Cryptogamic Flora of the Arctic: V. Bryophytes," *Botan. Rev.,* **20,** 425–450 (1954).

185. Stewart, G., Cottam, W.P., and Hutchings, S.S., "Influence of Unrestricted Grazing on Northern Salt Desert Plant Associations in Western Utah," *Jour. Agr. Res.,* **60,** 289–316 (1940).

186. Stickler, F.C. and Johnson, I.J., "Dry Matter and Nitrogen Production of Legumes and Legume Associations in the Fall of the Seeding Year," *Agron. Jour.,* **51,** 135–137 (1959).

187. Summerhayes, V.S. and Elton, C.S., "Further Contributions to the Ecology of Spitsbergen," *Jour. Ecol.,* **16,** 193–268 (1928).

188. Sylvén, N., "The Influence of Climatic Conditions on Type Composition," *Imp. Bur. Plant Genet., Herb. Plants Bull.,* No. 21, 1–8 (1937).

189. Tansley, A.G., "The Use and Abuse of Vegetational Concepts and Terms," *Ecology,* **16,** 284–307 (1935).

190. Tansley, A.G., "The British Islands and Their Vegetation," 2 Vols., Cambridge University Press, Cambridge, 1949.

191. Tedrow, J.C.F. and Cantlon, J.E., "Concepts of Soil Formation and Classification in Arctic Regions," *Arctic,* **11,** 166–179 (1958).

192. Thornbury, W.D., "Principles of Geomorphology," John Wiley & Sons, Inc., New York, N.Y., 1954.

193. Timmons, F.L., "The Rise and Decline of Cactus in Kansas," *Biennial Rept. Kansas State Board Agr.,* **33,** 37–46 (1941–1942).

194. Tisdale, E.W., "The Grasslands of the Southern Interior of British Columbia, *Ecology,* **28,** 346–382 (1947).

195. Tüxen, R., "Grundrisz einer Systematik der Nitrophilen Unkrautgesellschaften in der Eurosibirischen Region Europas," *Mitteil. Florist-Soziolog. Arbeitsgemeinschaft.,* **2** (N. F.), 94–175 (1950).

195A. Van Denack, Sr. Julia M. and Hanson, H.C., "The Danthonia-Lichen-Moss Community in Washington, D.C., and Vicinity," *Jour. Wash. Acad. Sci.,* **49,** 367–371 (1959).

196. Visher, S.S., "American Dry Seasons—Their Intensity and Frequency," *Ecology,* **30,** 365–370 (1949).

197. Watt, A.S., "Pattern and Process in the Plant Community," *Jour. Ecol.,* **35,** 1–22 (1947).

198. Weaver, J.E. and Clements, F.E., "Plant Ecology," 2nd Ed., McGraw-Hill Book Co., New York, N.Y., 1938.

199. Weaver, J.E. and Darland, R.W., "A Method of Measuring Vigor in Range Grasses," *Ecology,* **28,** 116–162 (1947).

200. Webb, D.A., "Is the Classification of Plant Communities Either Possible or Desirable?" *Botan. Tidsskr.,* **51,** 362–370 (1954).

201. Webster, C.B., "Meritorious Crop in War or Peace, Rescue Grass," *Southern Seedsman,* **7,** 11, 51 (1944).

202. Wells, P.V., "An Ecological Investigation of Two Desert Tobaccos," *Ecology,* **40,** 626–644 (1959).

202A. Whitman, W., Hanson, H.C., and Peterson, R., "Relation of Drouth and Grazing to North Dakota Range Lands," *N. Dak. Agr. Expt. Sta. Bull.,* **320,** 1–29 (1943).

203. Whittaker, R.H., "A Criticism of the Plant Association and Climatic Climax Concepts," *Northwest Sci.,* **25,** 17–31 (1951).

204. Whittaker, R.H., "A Study of Summer Foliage Insect Communities in the Great Smoky Mountains," *Ecol. Monographs,* **22,** 1–44 (1952).

205. Whittaker, R.H., "A Consideration of the Climax Theory: the Climax as a Population and Pattern," *Ecol. Monographs,* **23,** 41–78 (1953).

206. Whittaker, R.H., "Vegetation of the Great Smoky Mountains," *Ecol. Monographs,* **26,** 1–80 (1956).

207. Whittaker, R.H., "Recent Evolution of Ecological Concepts in Relation to the Eastern Forests of North America," pp. 340–358 *in* "Fifty Years of Botany," W. C. Steere, Ed., McGraw-Hill Book Co., New York, N.Y., 1958.

208. Wiersum, L.K. and Bakema, K., "Competitive Adaptation of the Cation Exchange Capacity of Roots," *Plant and Soil,* **11,** 287–292 (1959).

209. Wildeman, E.De., "Actes des III Congrès International de Botanigue," **I,** Gustav Fischer, Jena, 1910.

210. Wolfenbarger, D.O., "Dispersion of Small Organisms. Incidence of Viruses and Pollen; Dispersion of Fungus Spores and Insects," *Lloydia,* **22,** 1–106 (1959).

211. Woods, F.W. and Shanks, R.E., "Natural Replacement of Chestnut by Other Species in the Great Smoky Mountains National Park," *Ecology,* **40,** 349–361 (1959).

212. Wulff, E.V., "An Introduction to Historical Plant Geography," Chronica Botan. Co., Waltham, Mass., 1950.

213. Youngner, V.B., "Growth of U-3 Bermudagrass Under Various Day and Night Temperatures and Light Intensities," *Agron. Jour.,* **51,** 557–559 (1959).

INDEX

11; *rothrockii* (rothrock's G.), 106
Bracken. *See Pteridium*
Bramble, 37. *See also Rubus*
Braun-Blanquet, J., 81, 96, 126, 177, 179, 180
Brazil, 68
Briza media (Quaking grass), 36
Brockmann-Jerosch, H., 177
Bromegrass, smooth. *See Bromus*
Bromus (Bromegrasses)
    carinatus (mountain B.), 86; *catharticus* (rescuegrass), 92; *inermis* (smooth B.), 22, 23, 34, 35, 38, 51, 97; *marginatus* (mountain B.), 46, 93; *tectorum* (downy chess, cheatgrass, downy B.), 20, 47, 51, 73, 74, 88, 97, 101, 130, 131
Bryophyte community, 68
Buchloe dactyloides (Buffalograss), 11, 22, 23, 29, 46, 96, 102, 107, 110, 145
Buckeye. *See Aesculus*
Buffalograss. *See Buchloe*
Bulrush association. *See Scirpetum validi . association*

Cactus. *See Opuntia, Carnegiea*
Cakile, 56
Calamagrostis (Reedgrasses)
    montanenesis (plains R.), 84; *neglecta*, 16
Calamovilfa gigantea (Sandreed), 65
Calcification, 144
California, 20, 26, 36, 45, 57, 58, 61, 64, 68, 152
Calligonum comosum, 40
Calluna vulgaris (Scotch heather), 72, 143, 144, 157
Calochortus aureus (Mariposa lily), 88
Caltha palustris (Marsh marigold), 87, 95
Canada, 69, 73, 139
    British Columbia, 98, 99
    Quebec, 83
Canary Islands, 43
Candolle, A. de, 176
Carbón scrub, 64
Carex (Sedges)
    bigelowii (Bigelow's S.), 17, 64; *eleo-*

charis (needleleaf S.), 23; *filifolia* (threadleaved S.), 44, 70, 84, 99, 144; *misandra* (short-leaved S.), 16; *pennsylvanica* (yellow S.), 24, 94; *rupestris*, 139; *stenophylla* (needleleaf S.), 70, 84, 144
Caribou, 63, 162
Caricetum strictae association (Sedge association), 180
Carnegiea gigantea (Saguaro), 79
Carotene, 111
Carpetgrass (*Axanopus compressus*), 35
Carpinus (Hornbeams), 162
    betulus (European H.), 181; *caroliniana* (blue beech), 83
Carrying capacity, 110
Cassia eremophila (Partridge pea), 36
Cassiope tetragona (Four-angled mountain heather), 36, 187
Castanea dentata (Chestnut), 50, 51, 101, 142
Cation-exchange capacity, 31
Cattail marsh, 97, 140. *See also Typhetum association*
Ceanothus spp. (Bluebrush), 64
Central America, 64
Cerastium arctium (Arctic chickweed), 34
Ceratostomella ulmi (Dutch elm disease), 62
Cercis canadensis (Redbud), 83
Cercocarpus montanus (Mountain mahogany), 23, 185
Cetraria (Lichens)
    cucullata, 63; *islandica*, 18, 63; *nivalis*, 18, 61
Chamaephyte, 94
Change, classification of, 136, 163
    cyclic replacement, 21, 136, 144, 145, 146, 153, 155, 162, 163, 165
    directional, 125, 136, 140, 146, 147, 149–156, 159, 163, 164, 165, 166
    fluctuation, 136, 146–148, 159, 162, 163, 165, 166, 167
    in space, 136, 139, 156–158, 163
    in time, 135, 140
    intercommunity cyclic, 145, 146, 155, 163, 165, 166
    intracommunity, 145

Faber, von, F. C., 186
Factor. *See* Environmental factor
Fagus (Beeches)
  grandifolia, 83; *sylvatica* (European
    B.), 87, 187
Fauna, 186
Faunistics, 187
Fescue. *See Festuca*
Festuca-Agrostis grassland, 35
Festuca (Fescues)
  arizonica (Arizona F.), 47, 102, 108,
    184; *idahoensis* (Idaho F.), 45; *oc-
    toflora* (six-weeks F.), 11, 93; *ovina*
    (sheep F.), 21, 47, 62, 72, 139,
    158; *ovina* var. *duriuscula* (hard
    F.), 62; *rubra* (red F.), 187; *vivi-
    para* (viviparous sheep F.), 41
Fidelity, 103, 119, 126–128, 179
  classification of, 126
  definition, 126
Fir. *See Abies*
Fir, Douglas. *See Pseudotsuga*
Fire, ecological effects, 8, 41, 152
Flora, 186
Floristic composition, 66, 78–82
  use in classification, 178–181
Floristics, 187
Fluctuation. *See* Change, fluctuation
Fomes ignarius, 52
Ford, E. B., 43
Forest, classification of, 177, 185, 187
  coniferous, 80, 83–84
  deciduous, 51, 80, 83, 94, 101
  replacing grassland, 68
Formation, 66, 187
Frequence, Raunkiaer's law of, 113
Frequency, 78, 112–119, 129, 161,
    172, 178
  and pattern, 131
  percentage, 112
  use in biological spectrum, 95
Frequency-abundance index, 115–116

Galeopsis (Hemp nettle)
  bifida, 41; *tetrahit,* 41
Gaultheria procumbens (Wintergreen), 84
Gaura coccinea (Butterfly weed), 71
Gebietsassoziation, 181
Gene pool, 175

Genetic continuity, 61
Genotype, 15, 24, 42, 43, 92
Geographical characteristics, 177, 186
  use in classification of communities,
    186–187
Geographical distribution, 186
Geographical range, 128
Geological processes, 157
Geophyte, 93
Georgia, 35, 52
Germination, 65, 74
Glaciation, 138, 158
Gleason, H. A., 67
Glocladium, 37
Goldenrod. *See Solidago*
Good, R., 15
Goosefoot. *See Chenopodium*
Gradient, continuous, 141
  discontinuous, 141
  in environmental conditions, 69, 73,
    137–141, 156, 157, 167, 183
  intrastand, 139
  macro-, 139, 141
  medium scale, 138
  meso-, 141
  micro-, 139, 141, 157
  secondary, 138
Gramagrass-needlegrass-sedge com-
    munity type, 70–71
Grass-heath, 158
Grasshoppers, effects of, 49
Grasslands, 40, 53, 67, 81, 82, 94, 99
  biomes, 68
  California, 61, 68
  classification of, 177, 179, 185
  depleted, 90
  duration of, 44
  evolution of, 24
  frequency in, 114
  good condition, 31
  grazed *vs.* virgin, 115
  Great Plains, 72, 92, 96, 98, 140
  mature, 82, 128
  research in, 81, 102, 109
Grayia spinosa (Spiny hop-sage), 85
Grazing, and cover, 102
  and frequency ratio, 114
  and height of plants, 107, 108
  and weight of plants, 109–111

gradient, 164
in distribution of species, 116
morphological, 131
physiographic, 131
snow-field, 157
Pedicularis canadensis (Lousewort), 128
Penicillium notatum (Mold), 37
Pennsylvania, 33, 163
Penstemon parryi (Pink penstemon), 88
Perennial ryegrass. *See Lolium*
Periodicity, 77, 85–90, 119, 173
Permanence of communities, 158, 159, 164
Phacelia bipinnatifida (Phacelia), 80
Phalaridetum arundinaceae association (Reed canarygrass association), 180
Phanerophyte, 94
Phases, vegetation, 166
downgrade, 139, 153, 155, 162
upgrade, 139, 155, 162, 165
Phenology, 20, 28, 85, 90
Phenotype, 15, 27, 92, 96
Phippsia algida (Phippsia), 34, 58
Photosynthesis, 1
Phragmitetum communis iowenses association (Reed association), 180
Physocarpus monogynus (Ninebark), 185
Physiognomy, 66, 67, 121, 141, 142, 159, 177, 185–186
and pattern, 130–132
basis of classification of communities, 171, 173, 177, 186
definition, 130
Physiography, 132, 181, 186
Phytocenose, 66
Phytodecta americana (Defoliating beetle), 52
Phytoedaphon, 93
Phytoplankton, 93
Phytosociology, 66
Picea (Spruces)
engelmanni (Engelmann S.), 84, 187; *mariana* (black S.), 84; *sitchensis* (Sitka S.), 150
Pinus (Pines), 37, 38
banksiana (jack P.), 84, 150; *canariensis* (Canary P.), 43; *caribaea* (slash P.), 24; *contorta* var. *murrayana*

(lodgepole P.), 41; *edulis* (pinyon), 187; *jeffreyi* (Jeffrey P.), 13; *palustris* (longleaf P.), 35; *ponderosa* (ponderosa P.), 13, 137, 183, 184, 187; *resinosa* (red P.), 28, 64; *silvestris* (Scotch P.), 17, 62; *strobus* (eastern white P.), 62; *virginiana* (scrub P.), 155
Pinyon. *See Pinus edulis*
Pitcher plant (*Sarracenia flava*), 65
Plantago (Plantains, Indian wheats)
argyrea (I. w.), 88; *elongata* (slender P.), 144; *purshii* (wooly I. w.), 84
Plasticity, 8
Pleistocene, 56
Poa (Bluegrasses), 47, 88, 97, 98
alpina vivipara (viviparous alpine B.), 34; *bulbosa* (bulbous B.), 41; *macrantha,* 149; *pratensis* (Kentucky B.), 15, 35, 48, 97, 98; *pratensis* (Merion strain), 51; *secunda* (Sandberg B.), 98, 104
Point-contact method, 103
Point-observation plot, 103
Pollination, 27, 38
Polygons in vegetation, 158
Polygonum (Knotweeds)
erectum (erect K.), 144; *viviparum* (alpine Bistort), 16
Polytrichum (Moss), 84
Ponderosa pine. *See Pinus*
Ponderosa pine zone, 163
Poore, M. E. D., 173
Population
and ecological amplitude, 48
and genetic homogeneity, 24, 41, 42
and habitat, 137, 140
and number of individuals, 43, 100, 160, 163
changes in, 140, 166
definition, 1
Population density, 78, 100–101
and frequency, 113, 116–117, 118
and herbage area, 103
and volume, 111–112
Populus (Poplars)
sargentii (Great Plains cottonwood), 41; *tremuloides* (aspen), 40, 41, 53
Potentilla sterilis (Cinquefoil), 181